Church
Kitchen
Handbook

Church Kitchen Handbook

**Recipes and Menus • Planning and Equipment
Meditations and Prayers • Ordering Supplies
Staffing and Volunteers • Buffet Serving**

by

Marilee Mullin-Marshall
and
Virginia Meers

Illustrations by
Barry Luks

Publishing House
St. Louis

Copyright © 1985 Concordia Publishing House
3558 South Jefferson Avenue, St. Louis, MO 63118
Manufactured in the United States of America

Library of Congress Cataloging in Publication Data

Mullin-Marshall, Marilee, 1945-
Church kitchen handbook.

1. Quantity cookery. 2. Kitchens. 3. Church
entertainments. I. Meers, Virginia, 1919-
II. Title.
TX820.M851985642'.584-15573
ISBN 0-570-03944-4

1   2   3   4   5   6   7   8   9   10   KK   94   93   92   91   90   89   88   87   86   85

DEDICATION OF SERVICE

Lord . . . we ask that You be present with us in this place.

Make our activities a reflection of Your grace.

With humble hearts we petition that our labors be covered by Your mercy.

Keep us mindful of your peace when our work begins to look like chaos.

Give us all a willing spirit, able to accept direction with grace or to give it with meekness.

Discipline us with an appreciation of what it means to be a good steward.

Give us the fullness of joy as we present our labors as a gift acceptable to You, which is our reasonable service. Amen

Marilee

CONTENTS

PREFACE

Food and fellowship have always been a central part of the church's life. From the Upper Room to the church basement, there has often been a feeling of closeness as the people of God have come together to share a common meal.

Quite possibly, you are the one who has been selected to see that this tradition continues in your church. You may be anxious. Preparing a dinner for a large group is quite different from preparing one for your family. Where can you go for help?

That is the reason for the *Church Kitchen Handbook*. If you will look through its pages, you will find information dealing with all aspects of food preparation that will equip you for this important task.

Virginia Meers is an outstanding chef. She was one of the first women to be accepted into the American Academy of Chefs and educated at the Andrews School in Willoughby, Ohio. For 12 years she was the Food Service Director at the Mt. Hermon Christian Conference Center in Mt. Hermon, California, where in the summer months she prepared up to 3,000 meals a day.

I hope that this book will add many exciting times to your church events. Praise God who has given us so much of His bounty, and may you be blessed as you serve in this important aspect of the church's life.

Marilee Mullin-Marshall

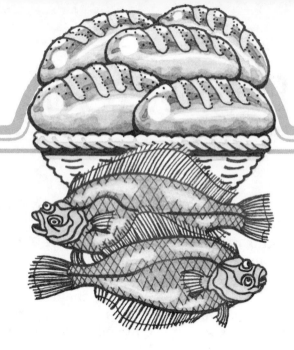

1 BEFORE YOU COOK

"Whether you eat or drink or whatever you do, do it all for the glory of God."

—St. Paul in 1 Corinthians 10:31

Our Lord is the Lord of miracles. With five barley loaves and two fish, He was able to feed a multitude. If you are in charge of cooking for an organization within your church, you may feel that you have been called upon to perform a miracle too. If so, the *Church Kitchen Handbook* is for you.

This book is designed to help remove the pressures of your task. Familiarize yourself with its contents. Enjoy the meditations, prayers, and Scriptures, which can turn an awesome task into a meaningful time of special closeness to the Lord.

Remember that the work before you is important. It does not matter whether you are the person in charge of the banquet project or a member of the cleanup crew, you are performing a service for the Lord, using the gifts and talents He has given you. Paul writes in Romans 12:6-8: "We have different gifts, according to the grace given us. If a man's gift is prophesying, let him use it in proportion to his faith. If it is serving, let him serve; if it is teaching, let him teach; if it is encouraging, let him encourage; if it is contributing to the needs of others, let him give generously; if it is leadership, let him govern diligently; if it is showing mercy, let him do it cheerfully."

As you begin this task of Christian service for the Lord, offer your hands and talents to Him for His use. Lean upon Him for support and direction as you would in any aspect of the Christian life. Use this opportunity to serve as a witness of God's love in your life. And may God, who is faithful to all His promises and loving toward all He has made, bless your efforts beyond measure.

CHAIN OF COMMAND

The Scriptures state that God is not a God of chaos, but of order. Paul's words "everything should be done in a fitting and orderly way" (1 Corinthians 14:40), although originally an admonishment to the Corinthians about their worship life, also apply to the kitchen. Someone has to take charge there—not as a slave driver or an autocrat, but as a leader aware of the needs to be served and the best means to achieve that end. That person is you.

Just as a captain must be in charge of a ship if it is to function effectively, you must assume the same responsibility in the galley. It is up to you to assign tasks and to see that they are carried out. Of course, this is to be done in Christian love. As you commit your work to the Lord, begin

to get your priorities in order. You will need to

1. plan the menu;
2. decide how much help you will need to serve the meal and the resources available for recruiting it;
3. decide what materials you will need in addition to those already available in the church kitchen;
4. determine where you can obtain food in quantity for the best price; and
5. decide how you can do all of this within your budget.

RECRUITMENT OF HELPERS

Once you have decided what type of meal you plan to serve, you must consider the amount of time needed for food preparation and how many people you will need to help you with the task. The axiom "many hands make light work" is not always true in a crowded kitchen. It is a real challenge to plan a big meal and to supervise its preparation in such a way that your helpers will not be tripping over each other. So, when recruiting volunteers, follow these basic principles:

1. Find people who carry assignments through to completion. Be careful not to assign a lot of tasks to a single person. You do not want frustration.

Give an assignment; see that it is carried out; give praise and thanks; and then either assign a new task or dismiss the worker.

2. Find people who *listen* to what you say. Not communicating properly is a problem in most of life; the kitchen is no exception. When you give directions, ask your helper to repeat them to you. This probably sounds silly, but in some cases it may save a meal.

3. Find people who are followers. You are the one in charge. You need helpers who will follow your directions. Finding such people will cut down on duplication of duties and help avoid hurt feelings.

4. Find people who are *not* good conversationalists. Of course, you want to have fun. There should be a feeling of loving and caring in the kitchen, but your primary concern is to get the meal done on time and done right.

5. Find people who are personally clean and tidy in appearance. Clean hands are a necessity in food preparation. People do not want to find a hair in the salad at a church banquet anymore than they would at a restaurant.

6. Find people who are aware that a kitchen requires self-discipline. It is not a place to take care of personal needs, such as combing one's hair. Also dress is important. You and your helpers should not wear your best clothes in the kitchen. Avoid loose-fitting articles that may catch on fire when you reach across a burner.

7. Find people who are coordinated. Health and fire hazards are *real* threats in a kitchen. There is a lot of activity going on in the kitchen at all times. Watch for potential dangers. When they arise, diplomatically reassign the person or persons involved to activities outside the kitchen. Also *never* let children run loose in a kitchen.

8. Find people who are goal oriented. The meal is not over until the last guest has left and the kitchen is clean. There are premeal preparations, things to be done during the meal, and things to do after the meal. *All* tasks are important. The church of Christ has been compared to a body where each part fulfills its functions for the good of the whole body. The same is true in the kitchen. Those who wash the dishes are just as important as those who set them out in the first place. The person who prepares the salad is just as important as the person who prepares the main course. Each person's goal is to complete correctly and on time the item which is his or her responsibility.

Now that you know *who* you want to help you in the kitchen, *where* do you find them? Here are some places to begin:

1. Your church bulletin. Ask for

volunteers. Assign them functions they can handle effectively and efficiently.

2. The telephone. Use your instincts and judgments. Service in the kitchen can be an outreach ministry. It should be nonthreatening; with direction, almost anyone can wash a dish or set a table.

3. The youth of the church. Although you should avoid the young child, there are teens who would be willing to help. Do not be afraid to ask boys as well as girls.

Remember, you need people who will work with you, not against you. Watch for the development of talents among your helpers. Adjust your plans so that you can utilize their abilities to the best advantage.

GETTING IT ALL TOGETHER

After you have planned the menu, after you have recruited your workers, after you have made an inventory of things on hand and things needed, take the time to put all the pieces together.

Take a sheet of paper and start planning. Assign tasks and note your strategy. The key to the completion of any project is preparation.

Remember your work is a sacred trust from the Lord. You are caring for the needs of God's people. Handle them with love. It is not an easy task. Prayer belongs in the kitchen. Ask the Lord for direction and insight to use your hands for the glory of His kingdom.

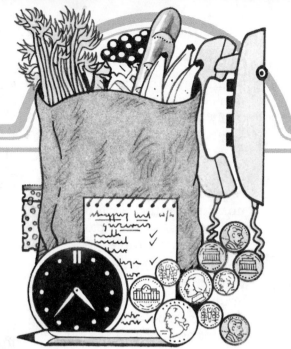

2 STEWARDSHIP IN THE KITCHEN

THANKS FOR SIMPLE THINGS

We thank Thee, Lord,
   for simple things,
The beauty of the common day
For every kindly word and deed,
For little griefs along the way.

We thank Thee for our home
   and friends,
For bounteous harvests and for bread,
And for the miracle of rain,
The bright sun shining overhead.

We thank Thee for the songs of birds,
For every night of peaceful rest,

But most of all we thank Thee, Lord,
That with Thy nearness we are blest.

From *Always in Christ*, copyright © 1961 by Concordia Publishing House, p. 82.

Stewardship, a word that you hear from the pulpit or read in a book, involves the responsible care and administration of the goods and duties entrusted to one's care. It is a combination of three factors: the giving of one's finances, the giving of one's time, and the giving of one's talents. The principle of stewardship also applies to the kitchen.

If you are not careful, there can be a tremendous waste of money, time, and talent in meal planning and preparation. The information provided in this and the following two chapters, however, will aid you in becoming a wise steward, able to exercise responsible care over the goods and duties you are in charge of.

First of all, before running down to the supermarket with your checkbook and your grocery list, find out how much money is being allotted to provide a meal. You cannot buy steak with a hot dog allocation. To stretch your dollars, keep in mind public resources. It is amazing what resources are available to nonprofit organizations if those in charge will only ask. For instance, supermarkets will sometimes give you a discount on your purchases with them, particularly on produce and meat, even to the extent of donating a portion of it.

Become familiar with your telephone yellow pages, looking at listings under Food Products or Food Service Suppliers. These businesses can supply large amounts of goods in more convenient sizes at lower rates—and probably deliver them too. Do not hesitate to ask for bids on food purchases. You are using the Lord's money, and wholesalers have a variety of price ranges as well as sometimes competing against other suppliers' prices.

Meat is the most expensive item on the menu. Shop around. Get to know your butchers. Often they may have an excess of one cut of meat that can be sold at a special price in bulk. Be flexible in altering your menu if you stumble onto a real bargain.

The following tables will help you in ordering for your needs by clarifying the wholesaler's terminology. What a case in peas means to a frozen food supplier means something entirely different to a frozen meat dealer. Be vigilant in comparing what you sign a delivery receipt for and what you do in fact receive. Plan on delivery errors, and be prepared with alternatives when the worst happens by keeping a "what if . . . " plan in the back of your mind.

SAMPLING OF VOLUME-PACKAGED PRODUCTS

ITEM	WEIGHT OR MEASURE PER UNIT	SERVINGS PER UNIT
BAKER'S GOODS		
Danish dough	2 sheets (13 1/2 pounds each)	9 3/4 dozen bear claws per sheet
Frozen biscuits	9 pounds per case	10 dozen
Frozen bread dough	22 1/2 pounds per case	60 loaves (6 ounces each)
Parkerhouse rolls	20 pounds per case	20 dozen
Pastry dough	26 1/2 pounds per case	9 3/4 dozen
DESSERTS		
Cakes (mix)	6 boxes (5 pounds each) per case	80 servings per box
Coffee cakes/muffins	6 bags (5 pounds each) per case	80 servings per box (cake)
		72 servings per box (muffins)
Cream puffs		72 per case
Eclairs		48 per case
Pies	6 pies (10 inches each)	48 servings
Pudding	6 cans (6 pounds each) per case	25 servings per can using #10 scoop
		30 servings per can using #12 scoop
Tart shells	1 1/2 pounds per case	160 servings
Turnovers	6 boxes per case (24 in each box)	144 servings total
DAIRY PRODUCTS		
Butter	30 pounds per case	90 prints per pound (individual servings)
Margarine	30 pounds per case	90 prints per pound
Cheese		
Cottage	5 pounds per tub	20 servings using #8 scoop
		25 servings using #10 scoop
		30 servings using #12 scoop
		40 servings using #16 scoop
		45 servings using #18 scoop
Cream	blocks (3 pounds each)	48 servings (1 ounce each)
Natural cheddar	blocks (40 pounds each)	640 servings (1 ounce each)

ITEM	WEIGHT OR MEASURE PER UNIT	SERVINGS PER UNIT
Parmesan	25 pounds, grated	400 servings (1 ounce each)
Processed	20 pounds per case	320 slices (1 ounce each)
Milk		
Half gallons	9 per case	72 cups (8 ounces each)
Quarts	16 per case	64 cups (8 ounces each)
Thirds	32 per case	32 servings (10 2/3 ounces each)
Buttermilk	16 per case	16 quarts
Half-and-half	16 per case	16 quarts
Ice cream		
Gallon tubs	3 gallons	96 servings (1/2 cup each or using #8 scoop
Novelties	box of 1 dozen	12 servings
Sherbet cups	box of 4 dozen	48 servings
Sundae cups	box of 3 dozen	36 servings
EGGS		
Fresh	2 boxes per case	180 eggs per box
Frozen	30 pounds per 3 1/2 gallons	160 servings (1 1/2 eggs each)
MEATS		
Beef		
Canned cubed beef	6 cans (6 1/2 pounds each) per case	
Hamburger, bulk	10 pounds per bag	40 portions (1/4 pound each or using #10 scoop)
Hamburger, 1/3-pound patties	10 pounds per case	30 portions (1/3 pound each or using #10 scoop)
Hamburger, 1/4-pound patties	10 pounds per case	40 portions (1/4 pound each or using #10 scoop)
Meatballs	10 pounds per case	160 portions (1 ounce each)
Skirt steak (cubed)	10 pounds per case	40 (1/4 pound each)
Tenderloin tips	10 pounds per case	40 (1/4 pound each)
Buffet		serves 7 people per pound
Family/women		serves 6 people per pound
Men		serves 5 people per pound
Top round roasts (30% shrinkage)	48 to 60 pounds per case (3 roasts, 15 to 20 pounds each)	220 servings (3 ounces each)

ITEM	WEIGHT OR MEASURE PER UNIT	SERVINGS PER UNIT
Hot dogs	10 pounds per case (2 or 4 ounces each link)	8 links (2 ounces each) per pound
Luncheon meat		
Bologna	1 roll (11 to 12 pounds)	176 servings (1 ounce each)
Pepper loaf	1 roll (6 pounds)	96 servings (1 ounce each)
Salami	1 roll (11 to 12 pounds)	234 servings (3/4 ounce each)
Pork		
Breakfast meat		
Bacon	10 trays per case	300 servings (2 pieces each)
Lil' smokies	10 pounds per box	25 servings (4 pieces each)
	45 pounds per box	112 servings (4 pieces each)
Link sausage	6 or 12 pounds per box	96 servings (2 pieces each)
Smokies	10 pounds per box	112 servings (2 pieces each)
Patties	12 pounds per box (128 pieces per box)	128 servings
Chops	10 pounds per case	
Diced	10 pounds per case	45 to 50 servings (5 servings per pound)
Ham		
Deli trim	6 cans (10 pounds each) per case	50 servings per can (3 ounces each)
Jubilee tavern ham	40 pounds per case (4 hams, 9 to 11 pounds each)	36 servings per ham (4 ounces each)
Veal patties	10 pounds per case	40 servings (1/4 pound each)
POULTRY		
Chicken		
Diced, frozen	5 or 10 pounds per case	
Eighths	96 pieces including wings	48 servings (2 pieces each)
Quarters	25 chickens per case	100 pieces
Airline breasts	24, 32, or 48 half breasts per box	6 ounces per serving
Turkey		
Diced	30 pounds per case (6 bags, 5 pounds each)	3 ounces per serving
Minibreasts	27 to 32 pounds per case (12 breasts)	3 ounces per serving (7 to 8 slices per pound)
Minithighs	35 to 40 pounds per case (3 thighs per pound)	3 ounces per serving

ITEM	WEIGHT OR MEASURE PER UNIT	SERVINGS PER UNIT
FISH		
Albacore	8 to 20 pounds per fish	1/2 pound (includes bones) per person
Cod	50 pounds per case (10 boxes, 5 pounds per box)	200 servings (1/4 pound each)
Salmon, boneless	5 pounds per box	6 to 8 ounces per person, raw weight
Sole, boneless	10 pounds per box	6 to 8 ounces per person, raw weight
Trout, boneless	30 pounds per case	6 to 8 ounces per person, raw weight
CEREAL		
Pastas and rice (dry)		
Noodles	10 pounds per box	200 servings family style
Rice	100 pounds per sack	7 pounds, using #12 scoop, serves 100
Spaghetti	20 pounds per box	7 pounds serves 100
Potatoes		
Instant mashed	6 No. 10 cans per case	100 servings (using #12 scoop) per can
Redi-shreds	6 boxes (5 pounds each) per case	45 servings per box
Sliced		100 servings per bag
VEGETABLES		
Canned	6 No. 10 cans per case	25 servings (1/2 cup each) per can
Fresh	daily changes	
Frozen:	30 pounds per case (12 boxes, 2 1/2 pounds each) *or*	200 servings (1/2 cup each
Broccoli		
Brussel sprouts	20 pounds per case bulk	200 servings (1/2 cup each)
Cauliflower		
Corn kernels		
French green beans		
Mixed vegetables		
Peas		
Spinach, etc.		
Corn cobbets	96 halves per case	96 servings (1 each)
Small whole potatoes	30 pounds per case (6 bags, 5 pounds each)	100 potatoes per bag
		25 servings (4 potatoes each)
		150 servings per case

19

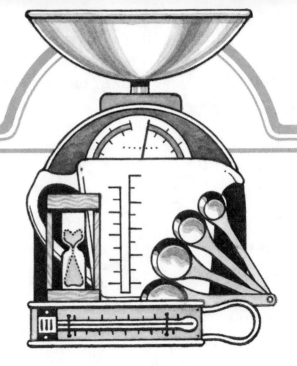

3 WEIGHTS, MEASURES, AND EQUIPMENT

LIQUID AND DRY MEASURE IN BIBLE TIMES

The smallest common unit for measuring liquids was the log. The Jews figured the log as the amount of water displaced by six hen's eggs, roughly the equivalent of our pint. Twelve logs made one hin, about 6 quarts, or 1 1/2 gallons. Six hins made one bath, about 9 gallons. The "firkins," mentioned in the story of the wedding of Cana (John 2:6), were about the same measure as a bath,

roughly 10 gallons. The largest measure was the homer or cor, the equivalent of 10 baths, or about 90 gallons.

Liquid measure

6 eggs = 1 log

12 logs = 1 hin

Units of dry measure were the following: The cab was somewhat under 2 quarts. Six cabs made one seah, not quite 10 quarts. Three seahs made one ephah, roughly the equivalent of a bushel. Ten ephahs made one homer, the largest common unit, about10 bushels. The Roman *modius,* translated "bushel" in Matt. 5:15, is really about a peck, one quarter of our bushel, a size very handy around the home.

From *Home Life in Bible Times,* copyright © 1947, 1969 by Concordia Publishing House, pp. 151-52.

TABLE OF WEIGHTS AND APPROXIMATE MEASURES

ITEM	WEIGHT	APPROX. MEASURE
APPLES	1 1/2 pounds	1 quart, sliced
APPLES	1 pound	1 quart, diced
APRICOTS, diced	1 pound	3 cups
APRICOTS, diced, cooked, no juice	1 pound	5 cups
APRICOTS, fresh	1 pound	8 apricots
AVOCADO	1 pound	2 medium
BACON, cooked, diced	1 pound	1 1/2 cups
BACON, uncooked, diced	1 pound	1 pint
BAKING POWDER	1 ounce	2 1/2 tablespoons
BAKING POWDER	1 pound	2 1/2 cups
BANANAS	1 pound	3 medium
BANANAS, mashed	1 pound	1 1/4 cups
BANANAS, sliced	1 pound	2 1/2 cups
BARLEY, pearl	1 pound	1 pint
BEANS, lima, dried	1 pound	2 2/3 cups
BEANS, lima, fresh	1 1/2 pounds	1 quart
BEANS, lima, 1 pound soaked and cooked	2 1/2 pounds	6 cups
BEANS, kidney, canned	1 pound	2 2/3 cups
BEANS, kidney, 1 pound soaked and cooked	2 3/8 pounds	7 cups
BEANS, navy, canned	1 pound	2 1/3 cups
BEANS, navy, 1 pound soaked and cooked	2 1/8 pounds	6 cups
BEEF, dried	1 pound	1 quart

ITEM	WEIGHT	APPROX. MEASURE
BEETS, young	6 pounds, net	1 dozen
BEETS, cooked, diced	1 pound	2 1/4 cups
BEETS, cooked sliced	1 1/2 pounds	1 quart
BRAN, ALLBRAN	8 ounces	1 quart
BRAN, flakes	1 pound	3 quarts
BRAN, unwashed	1 pound	4 quarts
BRAN, soft, broken	1 pound	9 cups
BREAD, stale, broken	1 pound	9 cups
BREAD, crumbs, dry	1 pound	5 cups
BREAD, crumbs, fresh	1 pound	2 quarts
BREAD CUBES, for topping	4 1/2 ounces	1 quart
BUTTER	1 ounce	2 tablespoons
BUTTER	1 pound	1 pint
CABBAGE, shredded	1 pound	5 1/2 cups
CABBAGE, shredded and chopped	1 pound	1 quart
CARROTS	1 pound	6 small
CARROTS, cooked, diced	1 pound	3 cups
CARROTS, raw, diced	1 pound	3 cups
CARROTS, raw, ground	1 pound	3 1/4 cups
CAKE CRUMBS, not dry	10 ounces	1 quart
CAULIFLOWER, 1 crate	12 1/2 pounds	10 quarts
CELERY, diced, cooked	1 bunch (1 pound)	1 1/2 cups
CELERY, diced 1/2-inch pieces	1 pound	4 1/2 cups
CELERY, diced 1/4-inch pieces	1 pound	4 cups
CHEESE, brick, 5 pounds	1 pound	16 thin slices
CHEESE, cottage	1 pound	2 1/4 cups
		8 servings (#10 dipper)
		12 servings (#16 dipper)
		25 servings (#30 dipper)
CHEESE, diced 1/4-inch cubes	1 pound	3 1/2 cups
CHEESE, grated or ground	1 pound	1 quart
CHEESE, Philadelphia cream	3 ounces	1/3 cup
CHERRIES, candied	1 pound	2 1/2 cups
CHERRIES, glacé	1 pound	96 cherries
CHICKEN, dressed	5 pounds	1 quart, cooked, diced
CHICKEN, dressed	5 pounds	1 1/4 pounds, cooked, boned
CHOCOLATE	1 pound	16 squares

ITEM	WEIGHT	APPROX. MEASURE
CHOCOLATE, grated	1 ounce	4 tablespoons
CHOCOLATE, grated	1 pound	4 cups
CHOCOLATE, melted	1 pound	2 cups
CITRON, dried, chopped	3 ounces	1 cup
CLAMS	1 quart	24 to 40 large
		40 to 60 medium
		60 to 100 small
COCOA	1 pound	4 cups
COCONUT, shredded	1 pound	7 cups
COFFEE, coarse grind	1 pound	4 3/4 cups
COFFEE, fine grind	1 pound	5 cups
CORN FLAKES	1 pound	4 quarts
CORNMEAL	1 pound	3 cups
CORN SYRUP	11 ounces	1 cup
CORN SYRUP	1 pound	1 1/3 cups
CORNSTARCH	1 ounce	3 tablespoons
CORNSTARCH	1 pound	3 cups
CRAB, whole	1/2 pound	1/2 cup meat
CRAB MEAT, flaked	1/2 pound	3 cups
CRACKERS, broken	1/2 pound	3 cups
CRACKERS, crumbs, fine	2 1/2 ounces	1 cup
CRACKERS, crumbs, fine	10 ounces	1 quart
CRANBERRIES, cooked	1 pound	1 quart
CRANBERRIES, raw	1 pound	4 cups
CRANBERRIES, sauce, jellied	1 pound	2 cups
CREAM OF TARTAR	1 ounce	3 tablespoons
CREAM OF TARTAR	1 pound	3 cups
CUCUMBERS, diced	1 pound	3 cups
CURRANTS	1 pound	3 1/4 cups
CURRANTS, dried	1 pound	3 cups
DATES	1 pound	2 1/2 cups
DATES, pitted	1 pound	3 cups
		50 to 60 medium dates
EGGS, hard cooked	1 pound	8 eggs
EGGS, hard cooked, chopped	1 pound	3 cups
FARINA, cooked	1 pound	3 3/4 quarts
FARINA, uncooked	1 pound	3 cups
FIGS, dry	1 pound	2 3/4 cups
		44 figs
FIGS, dry, finely cut	1 pound	2 1/2 to 3 cups
FLOUR, barley	1 pound	4 cups
FLOUR, cake, sifted	1 pound	4 cups
FLOUR, cracked wheat	1 pound	4 cups

Weights, Measures, and Equipment

ITEM	WEIGHT	APPROX. MEASURE
FLOUR, graham	1 pound	3 1/3 cups
FLOUR, rye	1 pound	4 cups
FLOUR, white, all-purpose	1 pound	1 quart
FLOUR, whole wheat	1 pound	1 quart
GELATIN, granulated	1 ounce	3 tablespoons
GELATIN, granulated	1 pound	3 cups
GELATIN, flavored	1 ounce	2 1/2 tablespoons
GELATIN, flavored	1 pound	2 1/2 cups
GIBLETS, cooked, trimmed, and cubed	1 pound	2 1/4 to 2 1/2 cups
GLUCOSE	1 pound	1 1/3 cups
GRAPEFRUIT, size 54	1	1 1/2 cups of sections
GRAPENUTS	1 pound	4 cups
GRAPES, cut, seeded	1 pound	2 3/4 cups
GRAPES, on stem	1 pound	1 quart
GREEN PEPPERS	1 pound	7 medium
GREEN PEPPERS, chopped	5 ounces	1 cup
GREEN PEPPERS, chopped	1 pound	3 1/8 cups
HOMINY GRITS, uncooked	1 pound	3 cups
HOMINY GRITS, 1 pound, cooked	6 1/2 pounds	3 1/4 quarts
HONEY	11 ounces	1 cup
HONEY, strained	1 pound	1 1/3 cups
HORSERADISH, prepared	1 ounce	2 tablespoons
JAM OR JELLY	1 pound	1 1/2 cups
LARD	1 pound	2 cups
LEMON JUICE	1 ounce	2 tablespoons
LEMON RIND	1 ounce	1/4 cup
LEMONS, size 300	1 pound	4 lemons
LEMONS, 1, size 300	1/4 cup juice	
	1 teaspoon rind	
LEMONS, 4 or 5, size 300	8 ounces	1 cup juice
LETTUCE, broken, 2-inch pieces	1 pound	1/2 gallon
LETTUCE, leaf	1 pound	30 to 40 leaves for salad garnish
LETTUCE, shredded	1 pound	1/2 gallon
MACARONI, 1-inch pieces	1 pound	1 1/4 quarts
MACARONI, 1 pound, after cooking	5 pounds	2 1/2 quarts

ITEM	WEIGHT	APPROX. MEASURE
MACARONI, cooked	1 pound	2 1/2 cups
MARSHMALLOWS	1 pound	2 quarts (102 whole)
MEAT, cooked, chopped	1 pound	2 cups
MEAT, cooked, cubed, or ground	1 pound	3 cups
MEAT, uncooked, ground	1 pound	2 cups
MILK	1 pound	2 cups
MILK, evaporated, No. 1 tall	14 1/2 ounces	1 2/3 cups
MILK, powdered	1 pound	2 1/2 cups
MINCEMEAT	1 pound	2 1/2 cups
MOLASSES	11 ounces	1 cup
MOLASSES	1 pound	2 cups
MUSHROOMS, sliced, fresh, fried	1 pound	1 1/2 cups
NOODLES, uncooked	1 pound	2 1/4 quarts
NOODLES, 1 pound, after cooking	4 1/2 pounds	3 1/2 quarts
NUTMEATS, sliced or chopped	1 pound	1 quart
OATS, rolled	1 pound	4 3/4 cups
OATS, rolled, cooked	1 pound	3 to 3 1/2 cups
OIL	7 1/2 ounces	1 cup
OLIVES, green, size 180 to 200	1 quart	109 to 116 olives
OLIVES, ripe, size 120 to 150	1 quart	152 olives
ONIONS	1 pound	4 to 5 medium
ONIONS, chopped	1 pound	3 cups
ORANGE RIND	1 ounce	1/4 cup
ORANGES, size 150	1 pound	2
	8 oranges	1 quart of sections
ORANGES, size 150	3 average size	1 cup juice
ORANGES, size 150, diced w/juice	3 pounds	1 quart
PARSLEY, chopped	3 ounces	1 cup
PARSLEY, finely chopped	1 medium bunch	1/4 cup
PARSNIPS	1 pound	4
PEACHES, dried	1 pound	3 cups
PEACHES, 1 pound, soaked and cooked without juice	2 1/2 pounds	
PEANUT BUTTER	1 pound	1 3/4 cups
PEAS, dried, 1 pound, after cooking	2 1/2 pounds	5 1/2 cups
PEAS, green or yellow, split	1 pound	2 1/4 cups

ITEM	WEIGHT	APPROX. MEASURE
PEAS, 1 pound		1 cup
PICKLE SWEET RELISH	1 pound	2 3/4 cups
PICKLES	1 pound	3 cups
PIMIENTO, canned, chopped	7 ounces	1 cup
PINEAPPLE, diced or tidbits	1 pound	1 pint
PINEAPPLE, fresh	2 pounds	2 1/2 cups
POTATOES, cooked, diced	1 pound	3 medium
POTATOES, mashed	1 pound	2 cups
POTATOES, sweet	1 pound	3 medium
PRUNES, dried, 1 pound	1 pound	32 to 40 prunes
PRUNES, 1 pound after cooking	2 pounds	4 cups
PRUNES, 1 pound, cooked, pitted	1 pound	3 cups
RAISINS, seeded	1 pound	2 1/2 cups
RAISINS, seeded, chopped	1 pound	2 cups
RAISINS, seedless	1 pound	3 cups
RAISINS, seedless, chopped	1 pound	2 cups
RHUBARB, cooked	1 pound	2 1/2 cups
RHUBARB, 1-inch pieces	1 pound	4 cups
RICE, uncooked	1 pound	2 cups
RICE, 1 pound, after cooking	3 pounds, 6 ounces	2 quarts
RUTABAGAS, cooked	1 pound	1 1/2 cups, mashed
		2 1/2 cups, diced
RUTABAGAS, raw, cubed	1 pound	3 1/3 cups
SALMON, flaked	1 pound	2 cups
SALT	1 pound	2 cups
SAUERKRAUT	1 pound	2 1/4 cups
SAUSAGE, link, small	1 pound	16 to 17
SHORTENING	1 pound	2 cups
SODA	1 ounce	2 tablespoons
SODA	1 pound	2 cups
SPAGHETTI, 2-inch pieces	1 pound	1 1/4 quarts
SPAGHETTI, 1 pound after cooking	1 pound	2 3/4 quarts
SPICES		
allspice, ground	1 ounce	4 1/2 tablespoons
caraway seed	1 ounce	1/4 cup
celery salt	1 ounce	3 tablespoons
celery seed	1 ounce	1/4 cup
chili powder	1 ounce	6 tablespoons

ITEM	WEIGHT	APPROX. MEASURE
cinnamon, ground	1 ounce	1/4 cup
cloves, ground	1 ounce	1/4 cup
cloves, whole	1 ounce	6 tablespoons
cloves, whole	3 ounces	1 cup
curry powder	1 ounce	1/4 cup
ginger, candied, cut 1/4-inch	1 ounce	3 tablespoons
ginger, ground	1 ounce	5 tablespoons
mace, ground	1 ounce	1/4 cup
mace, whole	1 ounce	7 tablespoons
mustard, ground	1 ounce	4 1/2 tablespoons
mustard, prepared	1 ounce	1/4 cup
nutmeg	1 ounce	3 1/2 tablespoons
paprika	1 ounce	4 tablespoons
pepper, black	1 ounce	3 1/4 tablespoons
pepper, red	1 ounce	3 1/2 tablespoons
pepper, white	1 ounce	1/4 cup
peppercorns	1 ounce	3 tablespoons
poppy seed	1 ounce	3 tablespoons
sage	1 ounce	1/2 cup
SPINACH, raw, chopped	1 pound	1 gallon
SPINACH, 1 pound raw, cooked	13 ounces	2 3/4 cups
STRAWBERRIES, when crushed	1 quart	2 1/4 cups
SUGAR, brown	1 pound	3 cups
SUGAR, cubes	1 pound	96 cubes
SUGAR, granulated	1 pound	1 pint
SUGAR, loaf	1 pound	80 to 90 pieces
SUGAR, powdered	1 pound	3 1/2 cups
SUET, ground	1 pound	3 1/2 cups
TAPIOCA, quick cooking	1 pound	2 3/4 cups
TAPIOCA, pearl	1 pound	3 1/2 cups
TEA	1 pound	6 cups
TOMATOES, fresh	1 pound	3 to 4 medium
TOMATOES, fresh, diced	1 pound	1 pint
TURNIPS	1 pound	2 to 3
TURNIPS, raw, diced	1 pound	1 1/2 pints
TUNA, flaked	1 pound	2 cups
VANILLA	1 ounce	2 tablespoons flavoring
VANILLA TABLETS	6 tablets	2 tablespoons flavoring
VANILLA TABLETS, imitation	1 tablet	1 teaspoon flavoring
VINEGAR	1 ounce	2 tablespoons
WATERCRESS	1 pound	5 bundles
WHITE SAUCE, medium	8 ounces	1 cup
YEAST, active dry	1/4 ounce	1 package
YEAST, compressed	1/2 ounce	1 cake

COOKING TIMES, METHODS, AND TEMPERATURES

ITEM	GRILL	CONVECTION OVEN	CONVENTIONAL OVEN
CASEROLES			
Cooked meat		1 hour/325°F	1 hour/350°F
Raw meat		1 1/2 hours/300°F	1 1/2 to 2 hours/325°F
Vegetable		45 minutes/325°F	1 hour/350°F
FISH			
Albacore		25 minutes/325°F	40 minutes/350°F
Cod		45 minutes to 1 hour/325°F	45 minutes to 1 hour/350°F
POULTRY			
Chicken (quarters)		35 minutes/325°F	40 minutes/350°F
Turkey		35 minutes per pound/325°F	40 minutes per pound/350°F
MEATS			
Beef			
Hamburger patties (1/3 or 1/4 pound each)	Quick brown while frozen.		
Roast (15 to 20 pounds)			8 to 10 hours/low (overnight).
Swiss steak	Dredge and brown.	NO!!!	1 1/2 to 2 hours/350°F
Tenderloin tips	Brown and cook.	1/2 hour/325°F	1 hour/350 to 400°F
Lamb			
Chops	Brown and cook.		
Leg		25 minutes per pound/300°F	25 minutes per pound/325°F
Pork			
Bacon, precooked		2 minutes/400°F	
Bacon, raw	Brown and crisp.		
Chops	Brown.	2 hours/325°F	2 hours/350°F
Ham, precooked		1 hour/200°F	1 1/2 hours/250°F
Hot dogs	Cook in steam chest for 10 to 15 minutes.		
Roast			25 minutes per pound/325°F
Sausage		1 hour/325°F	1 hour/350°F

	STEAM CHEST	STEAM KETTLE	STOVE TOP
RICE	1/2 gallon/35 to 40 minutes 1 gallon/45 to 50 minutes		Bring to boil; hold on simmer for 40 to 50 minutes, tightly covered.
EGGS			
Soft cooked	Turn on pressure for 5 minutes; stop.		Bring to boil; cover tightly and remove from heat. Allow to stand for 4 minutes; pour off water.
Hard cooked	Turn on pressure for 15 minutes; stop.		Same as above but allow to stand for 30 minutes.
Poached	Heat large pan of water to boiling; put in flat pan; drop in eggs. Slip into oven and bake covered for 5 to 8 minutes at 350°F.		
Scrambled	25 to 30 minutes (shallow) 40 minutes (deep)		Use a greased sauce or fry pan on low heat; stir frequently until soft done.
VEGETABLES			
Canned	5 minutes	Boil 1 minute.	Boil 1 minute.
Frozen			
Green beans		Boil 4 to 5 minutes.	Boil 4 to 5 minutes.
Broccoli	10 to 15 minutes	15 to 20 minutes	15 to 20 minutes
Carrots	1 minute	Boil 1 minute.	Boil 1 minute.
Corn kernels	1 minute	Boil 1 minute.	Boil 1 minute.
Corn cobbets	10 minutes		
Mixed vegetables	10 minutes	Boil 4 to 5 minutes.	Boil 5 to 6 minutes.
Peas	No	Bring near boil and turn off.	
Spinach	10 to 15 minutes	Boil 2 minutes.	Boil 2 minutes.

INTERNAL TEMPERATURES OF RARE, MEDIUM, AND WELL-DONE MEAT

ITEM	DEGREE OF DONE-NESS AT 325°F OVEN	INTERNAL TEMPERA-TURES	APPROXIMATE TIME
BEEF	rare	140°F	25 minutes per pound
	medium	160°F	28 minutes per pound
	well done	170°F	35 minutes per pound
LAMB	medium	165°F	30 minutes per pound
	well done	175°F	40 minutes per pound
PORK, fresh	well done	155°F	35 minutes per pound
PORK, cured, uncooked	well done	155°F	20 minutes per pound
PORK, cured, cooked	well done	155°F	10 minutes per pound
POULTRY	medium	165°F	20 minutes per pound
	well done	180°F	15 minutes per pound
VEAL, shoulder	well done	170°F	45 minutes per pound
VEAL, boned and rolled	well done		40 minutes per pound

MEASURING EQUIPMENT

LIQUID AND DRY MEASURES

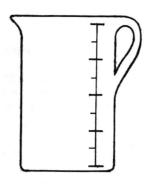

SIZE		EQUIVALENT MEASURE
1 gallon (gal.)	=	4 quarts
		8 pints
		16 cups
		128 fluid ounces

1 quart (qt.)	=	2 pints
		4 cups
		32 fluid ounces

SIZE		EQUIVALENT MEASURE
1 pint (pt.)	=	2 cups 16 fluid ounces
1 cup (c)	=	1/2 pint 8 fluid ounces 16 tablespoons 48 teaspoons
1/2 cup	=	4 fluid ounces 8 tablespoons 24 teaspoons
1/3 cup	=	2 1/3 fluid ounces plus 5 tablespoons plus 1 teaspoon 16 teaspoons
1/4 cup	=	2 fluid ounces 4 tablespoons 12 teaspoons

LADLES

SIZE (OUNCES)	EQUIVALENT MEASURE IN CUPS
1	1/8
2	1/4
4	1/2
6	3/4
8	1
12	1 1/2
16	2
24	3
32	4

SCOOPS

Scoops are numbered to indicate their size, which is determined by the number of scoopfuls it takes to make a quart. For example, it takes 16 scoops when using #16 scoop (1/4 cup) to fill 1 quart; or it takes 8 scoops of #8-size scoop to make 1 quart.

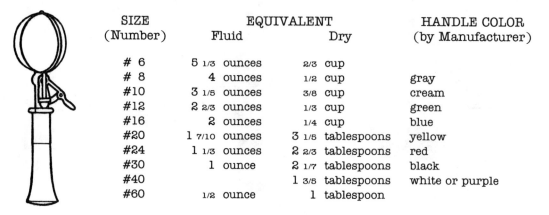

SIZE (Number)	EQUIVALENT Fluid	EQUIVALENT Dry	HANDLE COLOR (by Manufacturer)
# 6	5 1/3 ounces	2/3 cup	
# 8	4 ounces	1/2 cup	gray
#10	3 1/5 ounces	3/8 cup	cream
#12	2 2/3 ounces	1/3 cup	green
#16	2 ounces	1/4 cup	blue
#20	1 7/10 ounces	3 1/5 tablespoons	yellow
#24	1 1/3 ounces	2 2/3 tablespoons	red
#30	1 ounce	2 1/7 tablespoons	black
#40		1 3/5 tablespoons	white or purple
#60	1/2 ounce	1 tablespoon	

KITCHEN EQUIPMENT

STEAM TABLE COUNTER PAN; used for both preparing and serving food

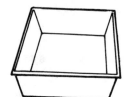

STEAM TABLE INSERT OR "BOOT-LEG"; used for soups and other liquids

BANQUET RING; used to keep food hot till served

STANDARD SHEET PAN; used for baking; most common size: 18x26 inches

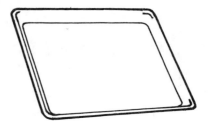

LAYER CAKE PAN; used for baking; most common diameter sizes: 7 inches, 8 inches, and 9 inches

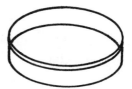

TUBE CAKE PAN; used for baking

CUPCAKE AND MUFFIN PAN

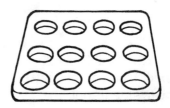

SAUCE PAN; for stove-top cooking; ranges in size from 1 to 10 quarts

SAUTÉ OR FRY PAN; sizes range from 7 to 14 inches

Weights,
Measures,
and
Equipment

HEAVY DUTY SAUTÉ PAN

OVEN ROASTING PAN; sizes: 16x20
inches and 18x24 inches

COLANDER; used to drain and rinse
food

CHINA CAP STRAINER; used to strain
food; often comes with hook to hang
over side of pot

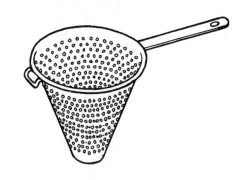

STOCK POT WITH SPIGOT

SAUCE POT for range-top cooking; comes in 6- to 60-quart sizes

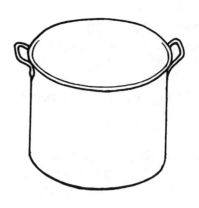

DOUBLE BOILER

BRAISER; used for braising and stewing; comes in 15- to 28-quart sizes

KNIVES

PIE KNIFE; used to remove pie wedges after cutting

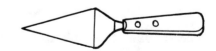

COOK'S FORK; used for handling solid items during food preparation work

ROAST BEEF SLICER; used to cut large cuts of meat; long and flexible

HAM SLICER; has a narrow blade and a flat tip

FRENCH KNIFE; used for slicing and chopping. The shape allows rocking of the blade without lifting the knife from the cutting board.

BREAD KNIFE

SCIMITAR STEAK KNIFE; used for cutting a large piece of meat usually when raw

SPATULA; used for spreading; flexible

BONING KNIFE; used to cut around the bones of meat to remove the flesh

PARING KNIFE; used for removing skins from vegetables

SANDWICH SPREADER; used to spread fillings

STEEL; used to straighten the edge of a knife; usually has a magnetized surface to pick up the steel burrs from the knife

SMALL FOOD SERVICE EQUIPMENT

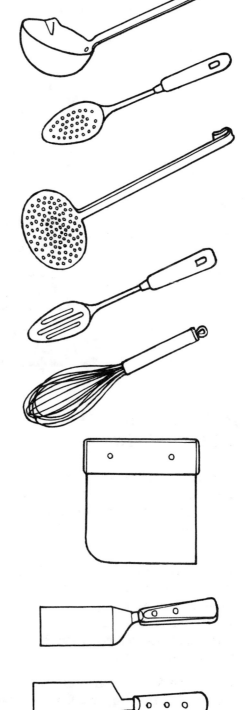

LADLE; used to remove liquid foods;
available in a variety of sizes

PERFORATED SPOON; used to drain
solid food when removing it from
liquid

SKIMMER; used to remove items
from deep fat frying or to remove
scum from stocks, sauces, etc.

SLOTTED SPOON; used to remove and
drain solid items from liquid

WIRE WHIP; used to mix foods by
hand

DOUGH CUTTER; used to divide yeast
doughs

SPATULA OR STEAK TURNER; used to
turn steaks or other items on a grill
or broiler

SPATULA OR HAMBURGER TURNER;
used to turn food on a grill

4 MENU PLANNING AND BUFFETS

TABLE PRAYERS FOR BEFORE MEALS

Come, Lord Jesus, be our Guest,
Our morning Joy, our evening Rest,
And with Your daily food impart
Your love and peace to every heart.
    Amen*

The eyes of all wait upon Thee, O Lord,
And Thou givest them their meat
    in due season;
Thou openest Thine hand
And satisfiest the desire of every
    living thing.

Our hands we fold, our heads we bow;
For food and drink we thank You now.

Be present at our table, Lord.
Be here and everywhere adored.
Thy children bless and grant that we
May live in fellowship with Thee.

Lord God, heavenly Father,
Bless us and these Your gifts
Which we receive from Your
    bountiful goodness,
In Jesus name. Amen

God is great and God is good;
Let us thank Him for our food.

Bless this food
Dear Lord, we pray.
Make us thankful every day.†

*From *Dear Father in Heaven,* copyright © 1963
by Concordia Publishing House, p. 12.

†From *Prayers for the Very Young Child,* copyright © 1981
by Concordia Publishing House, p. 32.

Feed Your children, God most holy,
Comfort sinners poor and lowly;
O You Bread of Life from heaven,
Bless the food You here have given.*

Come, Lord Jesus, be our Guest
And let Thy gifts to us be blessed.

*From *Dear Father in Heaven,* copyright © 1963
by Concordia Publishing House, p. 12.

MENU PLANNING

As you start to plan your menu, consider the group for whom you are cooking. Kids will not eat quiche, but love hamburgers. Women tend to favor salads and lighter dishes more than men. The meals that can be served are endless, but they must be tailored to the tastes of the group you are serving. And whatever menu you plan, keep it balanced both nutritionally and aesthetically, using colors, textures, and aromas that will please the eyes and nose.

As well as the tastes of the group, you must consider its size, the complexity of the menu, and the time element involved in preparing the food. Your space is probably limited too. Some things can be prepared ahead of time and brought to the kitchen; other dishes are best prepared at the serving site.

When planning your menu, also think about the order in which food should be scheduled for preparation. Although this is governed mostly by common sense, here are a few helpful suggestions. Appetizers are served first; therefore they can be prepared first. Most vegetables can be cleaned and cut as much as a day before cooking and stored in salted water in the refrigerator. Potatoes are an exception, however, since they can be stored in water only a few hours after peeling. Nevertheless, doing this is recommended as a timesaving measure. Mashing the potatoes and giving the meal its final seasoning is your last chore.

Meat can be sliced and served immediately only for small groups. It takes too much time and causes a backlog on other foods to do this for larger groups. A good policy is to cook and slice the meat the day prior to serving and store it under foil in the refrigerator. An hour before serving it, cover the meat in shallow pans, and heat.

The point to remember in food preparation is "get the food to the table with cold foods cold and hot foods *hot!*"

Finally, there is more to menu planning than writing words on a piece of paper. Your work is a service for the Lord. There are people to consider. So remember to be sensitive to personal relationships and feelings.

39

SAMPLE MENUS

BRUNCHES

Men:

1/2 Broiled Grapefruit with Cherry Garnish
Scrambled Eggs
Lil' Smokie Sausages
Biscuits
Butter and Jam
Coffee and Orange Juice

Women:

Cheese Soufflé
Virginia's Sour Cream Coffee Cake
Sausage
Orange Slice Garnish
Coffee and Pineapple or Grapefruit Juice

LUNCHEONS

Men:

Virginia's Meat Loaf
Mashed Potatoes and Gravy
Tossed Green Salad
Green Beans with Crisp Onion Rings
Oatmeal Cookies

Women:

Salad Bar
Three Dressings
Crusty Rolls and Butter
Fantastic Apple Macaroon Torte

or

Spinach Soufflé
Lettuce Salad
with
Mandarin Oranges and Slivered Toasted Almonds
Banana Bread and Butter
Fruit Crisp

KIDS' LUNCHES

I

Kids' Favorite Meat Rolls
Carrot Sticks
Potato Chips
Rocky Road Pudding
Milk

II

Do-It-Yourself Tacos
Refried Beans
Brownies
Milk

III

Hot Dogs
Macaroni Salad
Jello with Fruit
Chocolate Milk

BUFFETS

If a buffet is your serving plan, you will need one large table (using two lines, one down each side) for every 200 people. Below you will see three patterns of table arrangement for buffet service. The way in which you set up the table and arrange the food depends on the number of people to be served.

BUFFET TABLES

1 table, 8 ft. x 30 in.

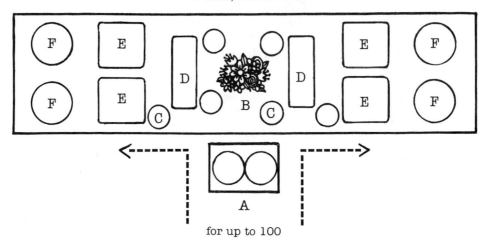

for up to 100

2 tables, end to end, 16 ft. x 30 in.

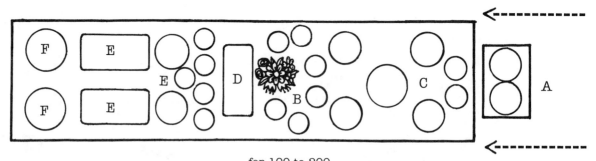

for 100 to 200

A. Plate Stacks
B. Decorative Arrangements
C. Cold Foods

D. Breads
E. Hot Foods
F. Meats and Entree

2 sets of tables, 16 ft. x 30 in.

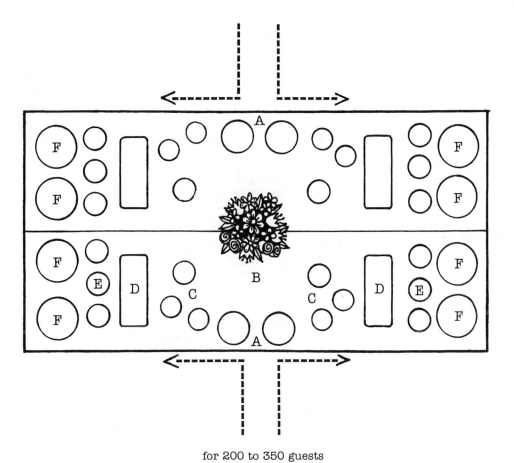

for 200 to 350 guests

BUFFET FOR 50

Tossed Salad (6 pounds)
Herb and Oil Salad Dressing (1 pint, page 79)
Pear and Cream Cheese (1/2 recipe, page 73)
Relish Plate
(2 pounds carrot sticks; 5 bunches radishes; 5 bunches green onions)
Pickles and Olives
Freckled Rolls (1/2 recipe, page 95)
Butter
Best-Ever Baked Swiss Steak (1/2 recipe, page 109)
Parsley Buttered Potatoes
Gravy
Carrots Julienne (7 pounds)
Chocolate Paradise Cake (1/2 recipe, page 154)
Coffee—Tea—Milk

BUFFET FOR 100 TO 150

Mandarin Salad (1 to 1 1/2 recipe(s), page 75)
Cranberry Salad (1 to 1 1/2 recipe(s), page 76)
Fresh Winter Relish Plate
(12 pounds total of cauliflower, broccoli, carrot sticks)
Sour Cream Dill Dip (1/2 gallon)
Ripe Olives
Virginia's Bona Fide Johnny Cake (2 recipes, page 94)
Butter
Elegant Glazed Chicken (1 to 1 1/2 recipe(s), page 128)
Rice Steamed in Chicken Broth (7 to 10 pounds)
Buttered Mixed Vegetables (13 to 20 pounds)
Baked French Custard (1 to 1 1/2 recipe(s), page 176)
Coffee—Tea—Milk

BUFFET FOR 200

Tossed Salad
Thousand Island Dressing (1 gallon, page 79)
Potato Salad (page 74)
Fruit Plate in Season
(spring—summer: citrus, banana, strawberry, melon;
fall—winter: citrus, banana, apple, grapes)
American Cheese Slices (1 ounce per person)
Mixed Sweet Pickles and Ripe Olives
Swedish Meatballs (page 110)
Braised Short Ribs with Zippy Sauce (page 110)
Whipped Potatoes
Buttered Peas and Onions
Oatmeal Muffins (page 90)
Butter
Rocky Road Pudding (page 178)
Coffee—Tea—Milk

COLD BUFFET FOR 100

Cold Sliced Cooked Meats
(32 pounds total of ham, meat loaf, turkey, roast beef)
Jarlsberg, Edam, Gouda, and Monterey Jack Cheese
(28 pounds sliced or served in rounds or chunks)
Cranberry Relish (12 cans)
Dijon or German Mustard (2 cups)
Cubed Butter (2 pounds)
Assorted Salads
(12 gallons total of coleslaw, potato, fruit, tossed green)
French or Rye Bread (6 loaves) or Rolls
Two-Layer or Tube Cakes (9 cakes, 9 inches each)
Beverages (28 cases or 12 ounces per person)

5 APPETIZERS AND BEVERAGES

PREPAREDNESS

"Abigail lost no time. She took two hundred loaves of bread, two skins of wine, five dressed sheep, five seahs of roasted grain, a hundred cakes of raisins and two hundred cakes of pressed figs, and loaded them on donkeys. Then she told her servants, 'Go on ahead; I'll follow you.' . . .

"When Abigail saw David, she quickly got off her donkey and bowed down before David with her face to the ground. She fell at his feet and said:

" '. . . let this gift, which your servant has brought to my master, be given to the men who follow you. Please forgive your servant's offense . . .' " (1 Samuel 25:18-28).

Dear Lord, help me to be as well organized in the kitchen as Abigail was, so that when the need to provide for others arises I'll be ready.

Make me as openhanded and generous as Abigail was when she gave bountifully to those who asked for help.

And Lord, just as Abigail averted a battle by her quick action in feeding David and his men, help me also to sow peace and to soothe feelings as I serve You in the kitchen. Amen

By Donna Crow

APPETIZERS

RUMAKI

Yield: 100 pieces

Ingredients:

- 4 pounds chicken livers, washed and halved
- 2 cups soy sauce
- 2 cups brown sugar
- 2 cups water
- 2 pieces (3 inches each) fresh ginger, sliced
- 4 sticks (2 1/4 inches each) cinnamon
- 4 garlic cloves, crushed
- 2 bay leaves
- 30 star anise*
  oil for frying
- 4 cans water chestnuts, halved lengthwise
- 48 bacon slices, halved crosswise

Combine all ingredients from soy sauce through bay leaves; slowly bring to a boil, stirring. Add livers and cook 2 to 3 minutes. Remove from liquid.

Assemble by wrapping a slice of bacon around 1 piece of liver and 1 slice of water chestnut. Secure with a toothpick.

Deep fat fry for about 1 minute or until the bacon is crisp. Drain and serve.

Star anise is found in the Chinese food section of most grocery stores.

HOT SHRIMP DIP

Yield: 100 servings

Ingredients:

> 2 cups finely minced onions
> 1/2 cup butter, softened
> 4 pounds cream cheese, softened
> 2 pounds shrimp, cooked and cleaned
> 1/2 cup lemon juice
> 2 teaspoons salt
> 1/2 teaspoon tabasco
> 2 teaspoons chili powder
> 2 teaspoons Worcestershire sauce
> 2 teaspoons garlic salt
> 2 tablespoons paprika

Use a food processor or grinder to chop onions; cook onions in butter over low heat until transparent. Put the butter-onion mixture in a food mixer. Add a heaping spoonful of cream cheese at a time until mixture is smooth. Add remaining ingredients except for the shrimp, which is gently folded in last.

Place mixture in chafing dish, hot pot, or other heating/serving device and bring it close to bubbling. Then reduce temperature, adjusting it to keep dip warm.

Serve hot with assortment of crackers (8 boxes).

HOT NACHOS

Yield: about 25 servings

Ingredients:

> 4 large bags corn chips
> 2 pounds grated sharp cheddar cheese
> 4 small cans jalapeño peppers, finely chopped

Place chips in a single layer on cookie sheets. Sprinkle lavishly with the grated cheese and less generously with the chili peppers.

Place under broiler until cheese melts. Serve hot.

ALTERNATE: Spread chip layer with canned refried beans before adding cheese and chili pepper layers.

CHEX PARTY MIX

Yield: 100 servings (easily)

Ingredients:

    3 1/2 cups butter (or part margarine)
        9 teaspoons seasoned salt
        7 tablespoons soy sauce
    1 3/4 teaspoons garlic powder
       14 cups Corn Chex (1 box)
       14 cups Rice Chex (1 box)
       14 cups Wheat Chex (1 box)
       14 cups Bran Chex (1 box)
        7 cups mixed salted nuts
        2 boxes pretzels

This needs to be mixed in batches unless you have a *very* wide-surfaced, deep pan.

GUACAMOLE DIP

Yield: about 15 cups

Ingredients:

       20 medium avocados, mashed
       10 large tomatoes, peeled and well chopped
      1/2 cup grated onion
    1 1/2 cups oil
      1/2 cup white wine vinegar
        1 tablespoon tabasco
        5 limes, juice only
        1 tablespoon crushed coriander (optional)
          salt and pepper to taste

Combine above ingredients. Dip can be used as it is, or for a smoother consistency process in blender.

Serve with corn chips or as sandwich spread.

CRAB RANGOON

Yield: 190 pieces

Ingredients:

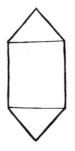
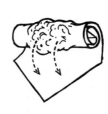

  1/2 cup sliced green onions
  1/2 pound crabmeat
  1/2 pound cream cheese
    1 tablespoon A-1 sauce
  1/2 teaspoon garlic salt
1 to 1 1/2 tablespoons lemon juice
      won ton wrappers

Combine above ingredients, except for wrappers. Place 1/2 teaspoon cream cheese mixture on corner of won ton square. Roll that corner up until only half of the wrapper remains loose. Using a beaten egg yolk like glue, put a small amount of yolk on one of the right or left corners. Now press the right corner over to the left and pinch together.

Deep fat fry until golden and crisp. Serve hot.

SUGGESTION: These could be made about 1 hour ahead and popped into a heated oven for 1 or 2 minutes to freshen.

VEGETABLE DIP PLATTER

Yield: 100 servings

Ingredients:

  3 pounds celery, cleaned, trimmed, and cut into 2-inch segments
  1 pound broccoli, cut into flowerettes, thicker stems cut horizontally across thickest part to make interesting flower shapes. If too tough, discard. If dull, parboil for 30 seconds in salted boiling water (or add lemon juice or vinegar to water instead of salt).
  5 pounds cucumbers, sliced (leave strips of skin on for extra color).
  3 pounds carrots, sliced diagonally or cut into sticks
  2 pounds zucchini, sliced or cut into sticks

ADDITIONAL VEGETABLES:

      radish flowerettes (Soak in salted ice water 1 day ahead.)
      cauliflower flowerettes
      cherry tomatoes

Vegetables can be prepared a day ahead of time if necessary. Store broccoli and zucchini in bags that are as airtight as possible. Store celery, cucumber, and carrots in containers of well-salted ice water.

Plan on using 1/2 gallon of sour cream dip with vegetable platter.

BEVERAGES

ORIENTAL JADE PUNCH

Yield: 200 servings (6 ounces each)

Ingredients:

- 4 gallons boiling water
- 2 cups green tea
- 4 cups sugar
- 6 cups frozen orange juice concentrate
- 1/2 cup fresh ginger
- 4 gallons grapefruit soda

Finely chop or mash fresh ginger and place in strainer or mesh ball. Pour boiling water over tea, add ginger, and steep for 5 minutes. Strain and add sugar; stir until dissolved. Chill.

When ready to serve, add soda.

TIP: Make ice cubes out of soda or fruit juice so they will not dilute the punch when they melt.

SUNSHINE PUNCH (YELLOW-GOLD)

Yield: 160 servings (1/2 cup each)

Ingredients:

> 3 quarts lemon juice
> 3 quarts orange juice
> 3 quarts sugar
> 3 quarts chilled water
> 3 gallons ginger ale

Mix sugar with fruit juices until dissolved. Add ginger ale just before serving.

SUGGESTION: Add 1 gallon of sherbet balls or garnish with mint leaves.

BLUSH PUNCH (PINK)

Yield: 120 servings (1/2 cup each)

Ingredients:

> 1 1/2 gallons water
> 4 cups sugar
> 4 cans (5 1/2 ounces each) frozen lemonade concentrate
> 2 quarts apple juice
> 1 gallon cranberry juice cocktail
> 1 quart orange juice
> 1 quart strong black tea

Heat water to boiling, stirring constantly until sugar dissolves. Add remaining ingredients. Chill.

APPLE PINEAPPLE PUNCH

Yield: 65 servings (6 ounces each)

Ingredients:

> 4 cans (46 ounces each) pineapple juice
> 2 1/2 quarts apple juice
> 1 gallon sparkling sweet soda

SPICED PINEAPPLE ORANGE PUNCH

Yield: 5 gallons (about 160 servings)

Ingredients:

        3   pounds sugar
        3   quarts water
        3   ounces cinnamon sticks
        4   teaspoons whole cloves
        8   cans (46 ounces each) pineapple juice
        3   quarts orange juice
    1 1/2   quarts lemon juice

Combine sugar, water, and spices. Simmer 30 minutes. Turn off heat and let stand 1 hour. Strain. Combine remaining ingredients. Chill well.

MT. CIDER MILL PUNCH

Yield: 100 servings (5 or 6 ounces each)

Ingredients:

        3   gallons apple cider
        3   quarts orange juice
        3   cups lemon juice
    1 1/2   cups honey
        6   sticks (1/2-inch each) cinnamon
       30   whole cloves
    1 1/2   teaspoons whole allspice
        3   tablespoons butter

Combine all ingredients in saucepan and bring
to a boil. Cover and simmer 1 hour. Serve hot or cold.

HOT SPICED CRANBERRY COCKTAIL

Yield: 160 servings (4 ounces each)

Ingredients:

- 1 1/2 quarts frozen orange juice concentrate
- 1 1/2 quarts water
- 1 gallon cranberry juice cocktail
- 2 teaspoons cinnamon
- 2 teaspoons nutmeg
- 2 teaspoons allspice
- 3 1/2 gallons ginger ale

Bring all ingredients except ginger ale to boil. Strain. Chill overnight.
Add ginger ale just before serving.

BOG FOG ON THE MOUNTAIN

Yield: 100 servings

Ingredients:

- 6 quarts plus 1 cup cranberry juice cocktail
- 6 quarts plus 1 cup orange juice
- 4 quarts weak lemonade
- ice

Mix juices and pour over ice.

SPECIAL TREAT: Omit ice and pour over a scoop of pineapple sherbet.

CHOCOLATE MOCHA

Yield: 5 gallons (about 100 servings)

Ingredients:

- 1 1/2 gallons strong, hot coffee
- 3 1/2 gallons hot chocolate

HOT CHOCOLATE

Yield: 80 servings (6 ounces each)

Ingredients:

    2 cups cocoa
    4 cups sugar
    2 tablespoons vanilla
  1/4 teaspoon salt
3 1/2 gallons milk

Mix cocoa and sugar together. Add remaining ingredients.

6 SOUPS AND SANDWICHES

THE BREAD OF LIFE

"Jesus said to them, 'I tell you the truth, it is not Moses who has given you the bread from heaven, but it is my Father who gives you the true bread from heaven. For the bread of God is he who comes down from heaven and gives life to the world.'

" 'Sir,' they said, 'from now on give us this bread.'

"Then Jesus declared, 'I am the bread of life. He who comes to me will never go hungry, and he who believes in me will never be thirsty' "(John 6:32-35).

Dear Father, the people I feed will be empty again so soon, and it will all have to be done over again. Thank You that You meet people's spiritual hunger conclusively.

As I labor to fill people's physical hunger, help me to do it in Your Spirit and to show Your eternal love in my work. Amen

By Donna Crow

___SOUPS___

CLAM CHOWDER

Yield: 6 gallons (100 servings at 8 ounces each)

Ingredients:

- 2 pounds butter
- 1 1/2 gallons chopped onions
- 1 cup flour
- 12 No. 5 cans clam juice
- 9 pounds potatoes, peeled and grated, or frozen hash browns
- 2 tablespoons salt
- 3 teaspoons white pepper
- 1 quart chopped clams
- 2 gallons half-and-half
- 2 quarts milk
- 2 dashes tabasco

Cook onions in butter until transparent. Add flour; cook, stirring constantly for 5 minutes. Slowly add clam juice, stirring to keep consistency smooth. Add remaining ingredients except for the half-and-half and clams. Simmer 30 minutes or until potatoes are tender. Add clams and light cream, and heat only until hot. Do not boil.

Garnish soup with chopped chives and serve.

CORN CHOWDER

Yield: 6 gallons (100 servings at 8 ounces each)

Ingredients:

  2 1/2 cups melted butter
    5 cups flour
    2 ounces chicken base
    2 gallons chicken stock
  1/3 cup salt
    2 tablespoons sugar
    4 cups diced onions
    4 cups diced celery
    4 cups cubed and cooked potatoes
    6 cups cream style corn
    2 gallons hot milk
    2 quarts buttermilk*

Mix flour with butter, and cook for 10 minutes. Add stock slowly, stirring constantly to keep consistency smooth. Add chicken base. Cook 15 minutes. Add vegetables, and cook 10 more minutes. Add corn, and cook 5 minutes longer. Add hot milk and buttermilk, and bring *almost* to boil. Taste for seasoning. Serve immediately.

CHICKEN CORN CHOWDER: Add chunks of cooked, coarsely diced chicken at the same time the cream style corn is added.

MEATLESS CORN CHOWDER: Omit chicken stock and base and use onion soup base instead.

Whole milk can be used as substitute.

GOLDEN CHEESE SOUP

Yield: 6 gallons (100 servings at 8 ounces each)

Ingredients:

>   6 cups finely diced celery
>   6 cups finely diced carrots
>   4 cups finely diced onions
>   3 gallons stock
>   3 cups melted butter
>   3 cups flour
>   3 quarts diced sharp cheese
>   3 gallons hot milk
> 1 1/2 teaspoons baking soda
>   1 tablespoon paprika
>   1 cup cornstarch
>   1/3 cup sugar
>   1/2 cup salt
> 1 1/2 cups cold milk
>   1/4 cup Worcestershire sauce

Simmer first 3 vegetables in 4 quarts of stock for 10 minutes. Add remaining stock and enough water to make about 12 quarts.

In separate pan blend flour with melted butter. Make roux and cook slowly for 10 minutes. Gradually add about 1 quart of hot stock to roux, mixing vigorously to keep smooth. Then slowly add this mixture to the pan containing the greater amount of stock mixture, stirring constantly. Lower heat to below boil; add cheese, allowing it to melt slowly while stirring it gently.

Heat milk. In separate bowl combine soda, paprika, cornstarch, sugar, and salt. Add cold water to make a thin paste. Stir into hot milk, and bring to simmer. Add Worcestershire sauce. Stir milk mixture slowly into cheese mixture, stirring constantly. Do not bring to boil. Taste for seasoning.

Garnish with chopped parsley.

NOTE: If soup curdles, it can be saved by processing it in the blender.

OLD ENGLISH LEEK AND POTATO SOUP

Yield: 6 gallons (100 servings at 8 ounces each)

Ingredients:

- 16 pounds leeks, sliced
- 12 medium onions, diced
- 1 pound butter
- 1 1/2 cups flour
- 4 gallons hot chicken stock
- 8 pounds potatoes, peeled and diced, or frozen hash browns
- 8 ounces chicken base
- 2 tablespoons salt
- 2 teaspoons white pepper
- 1 gallon half-and-half

Cook leeks and onions in butter until tender. Stir in flour, and cook 10 minutes, stirring constantly to keep smooth. Slowly add chicken stock, stirring with whip so roux is mixed in thoroughly. Simmer 10 minutes.

Add potatoes, and cook until tender. Add chicken base. Season with salt and pepper, and test to taste.

Just before serving, add warm half-and-half, being careful not to bring to boil as this will cause the soup to curdle.

Garnish with chopped chives.

OXTAIL SOUP

Yield: 6 gallons (100 servings at 8 ounces each)

Ingredients:

- 12 pounds oxtails
- 8 ounces fat
- 3 gallons beef stock
- 1 quart sliced onions
- 1 1/2 quarts diced carrots
- 1 quart diced celery
- 2 cups diced potatoes
- 2 cups barley
- 8 bay leaves

1 No. 10 can tomatoes
1 tablespoon salt (or to taste)
1 teaspoon pepper
1 teaspoon Worcestershire sauce

Brown oxtails in fat. Add remaining ingredients and simmer 4 hours. Strain out oxtails and vegetables. Pulverize vegetables and return them to the stock. Cut the meat off the bones and add them to the soup. As stock cools, skim off fat on surface. Before serving, reheat soup. Taste for seasoning.

PORTUGUESE BEAN SOUP

Yield: 8 gallons (100 servings at 10 ounces each)

Ingredients:

5 pounds ham hocks
4 pounds dried beans (any combination) *BlACK BEANS*
1 pound onions, diced
5 garlic cloves, peeled
3 quarts sliced celery, cut on diagonal
2 quarts diced carrots
1 No. 10 can tomatoes
2 pounds Portuguese sausage, cut into 1/4-inch slices

Place beans in pot, and cover with water. Bring to boil and allow to stand 1 hour after turning off heat. Drain.

Add ham hocks and onions. Cover with 5 gallons of water, and simmer covered until the meat falls off the bones. Remove bones and skin. Set meat aside to be diced. Add celery and carrots; cook until tender. Crush canned tomatoes and add to soup. Adjust seasoning to taste. Add diced ham.

Lightly cook sausage; add to soup just before serving.

VEGETABLE SOUP

Yield: 8 gallons (100 servings at 10 ounces each)

Ingredients:

> 5 gallons beef stock
> 4 quarts diced celery
> 1 quart diced onions
> 2 quarts diced carrots
> 1 No. 10 can tomatoes
> 1/2 cup salt
> 2 teaspoons pepper
> 1 quart green beans
> 1 quart canned kidney beans
> 2 bay leaves
> 1 clove garlic, crushed
> 1/2 teaspoon whole allspice
> 1 cup chopped parsley
> 1 quart frozen peas

Simmer all ingredients together except peas until tender, about 2 hours. Add peas and 1 more cup of chopped parsley. Heat for an additional 10 minutes.

TIP: For a delicious treat serve soup with a bowl of freshly grated Parmesan cheese on the side.

WHICH CAME FIRST: CHICKEN OR EGG SOUP

Yield: 120 servings (1 cup each)

Ingredients:

> 2 pounds margarine, melted
> 2 1/4 quarts flour
> 4 1/2 gallons chicken stock
> 2 ounces chicken base
> 3 cups chopped onions
> 3 green peppers, chopped
> 2 1/4 quarts diced celery
> 1/2 cup diced pimiento
> 1 teaspoon whole peppercorns
> 2/3 cup sugar

    2 1/2 gallons warm milk
      2/3 cup salt
       10 hard-cooked eggs, chopped
        2 cups cooked and cubed chicken meat
    2 1/2 quarts cooked rice

To margarine add flour; cook 10 minutes, making a smooth roux. Add chicken stock and base, stirring vigorously to keep smooth. Bring to boil. Add remaining ingredients from onions to (but not including) milk. Simmer 30 minutes.

Add milk. Heat but do not boil. Add chopped eggs, chicken, and rice; heat thoroughly.

Garnish with chopped parsley or chives.

_____SANDWICHES_____

BARBECUE SANDWICHES

Yield: 100 servings (3 ounces each)

Ingredients:

       19 pounds beef, pork, ham, or turkey, thinly sliced
    1 1/2 quarts Cowboy Barbecue Sauce (page 83)
    1 1/2 quarts gravy
        1 pound butter
      100 French, herb, or steak rolls

Partially split rolls in half lengthwise. Butter lightly. Prior to serving heat in oven until warm.

Blend meat with barbecue sauce and gravy. Heat until bubbly hot. For each serving place 3 ounces of barbecue meat on roll.

Serve with potato salad, dill pickles, and if in season, sliced red onion.

HAWAIIAN SURPRISE SANDWICHES

Yield: 100 servings

Ingredients:

6 pounds chicken, cooked and diced
6 pounds ham, finely diced
2 pounds celery, finely diced
2 quarts crushed pineapple, well drained
5 cups mayonnaise
2 cups finely chopped pecans
1 1/2 cups chopped green pepper
1/2 cup sliced green onion tops
salt and pepper to taste
4 to 6 tablespoons curry powder, or to taste
200 slices white bread
6 pounds (3/4 ounce per slice) Monterey Jack cheese (or 100 slices)

Mix curry powder with mayonnaise. Add remaining ingredients except for bread and cheese. Using a 1/2-cup measure or #8 scoop, place filling on sandwich bottoms. Top with slice of cheese and second slice of bread. Cover and chill.

When ready to serve, grill each side until brown. Hold in slightly warm oven until served.

OPEN-FACE BEEF MEDLEY
WITH BAKED TOMATO HALVES

Yield: 100 servings

Ingredients:

Baked Tomato Halves (below)

200 slices French bread
18 pounds roast beef, thinly sliced
6 pounds ham, sliced paper thin
9 pounds (1/2-ounce slices) mozzarella cheese
2 pounds butter
ripe olives

Allow 2 slices of French bread for each serving. Grill bread on one side. Spread ungrilled side with butter. Place 1 slice (1 1/2 ounces) of roast beef, 1 slice of ham, and 1 slice of mozzarella cheese on each slice of bread. Garnish with ripe olive. Place under broiler or in oven until cheese melts.

Serve with Baked Tomato Halves.

BAKED TOMATO HALVES

    6 cups fine bread crumbs
    1 cup grated Parmesan cheese
    1 tablespoon garlic powder
    2 teaspoons salt
  50 tomatoes, halved

Mix crumbs with enough butter to moisten. Add Parmesan cheese, garlic, and salt. Top each tomato half with 1 tablespoon of crumb mixture. Bake 10 to 12 minutes at 375 degrees F.

OPEN-FACE GUACAMOLE SANDWICHES

Yield: 100 servings

Ingredients:

      2 gallons finely diced avocados
      3 cups chopped green onions
  1 1/2 cups lemon juice
  2 1/2 tablespoons salt
  1 1/2 tablespoons pepper
  1 1/2 tablespoons garlic powder
      1 pound butter
  100 slices light rye bread
      3 gallons shredded lettuce
  200 tomato slices (about 10 pounds)
        Bleu Cheese Dressing (page 80)
  200 ripe olives
  200 bacon slices, fried until crisp

Combine avocados, lemon juice, and seasonings. Blend. Cover and chill until needed.

Butter bread (1 slice per sandwich). On each slice of bread place 1/2 cup shredded lettuce, 2 tomato slices, 1 #12 scoop of avocado mixture, and 1 #30 scoop of dressing. Top with 2 bacon slices and 2 olives.

Serve with refried beans topped with cheese.

SAUSAGE ROLLS

Yield: 100 servings (2 each)

Ingredients:

  20 packages (cans) flaky or buttermilk biscuits
2 1/2 cups horseradish dressing
1 3/4 cups German-style mustard
 200 smoked link sausages or smokie links

Roll out each biscuit on floured board to make a 3x6-inch rectangle. Mix horseradish and mustard together and spread each rectangle with 1 teaspoon of this mixture. Wrap 1 sausage in each biscuit, pinching edges of dough to make a seal.

Bake at 400 degrees F for 10 to 12 minutes.

BEEFEATER SANDWICHES

Yield: 100 sandwiches

Ingredients:

 200 slices dark rye bread (usually 16 slices per loaf)
      leaf lettuce
   2 pounds butter
  13 pounds beef, cooked and sliced paper thin
   3 quarts sour cream
1 1/2 cups dry onion soup mix
 1/2 cup horseradish
1 1/2 tablespoons salt
1 1/2 teaspoons pepper
   1 No. 10 can dill pickle slices (about 3/4 gallon)

Combine sour cream through pepper and let stand.

Butter 100 slices of bread and place a piece of lettuce on each. Put 2 ounces meat per sandwich on each slice. Use #40 scoop to put sour cream dressing on each sandwich. Top with remaining bread. Cover with plastic wrap and chill.

CHEESY MEAT ROLLS

Yield: 96 sandwiches (using #24 scoop)

Ingredients:

- 2/3 cup finely chopped onion
- 1 1/3 cups chili sauce
- 1 1/2 cups chopped green pepper
- 1 1/3 cup piccalilli
- 4 cups cooked and ground ham, beef, sausage, or Spam
- 4 1/2 quarts grated American cheese
- 96 hot dog buns, sliced

Combine all ingredients except hot dog buns and mix well. Using a #24 scoop, put 1 scoop of mixture into each hot dog bun. Place sandwiches in single layer on shallow baking pans. Cover with foil.

Heat at 350 degrees F for 10 minutes or until cheese has melted thoroughly.

KIDS' FAVORITE MEAT ROLLS

Yield: 96 sandwiches (using #24 scoop)

Ingredients:

- 2/3 cup finely chopped onion
- 1 1/3 cups mayonnaise
- 1 1/3 cups pickle relish
- 1/2 cup prepared mustard
- 1 1/2 quarts grated or ground Spam
- 4 1/2 quarts grated American cheese
- 96 hot dog buns

Prepare in same manner as Cheesy Meat Rolls.

FRENCH SEAFOOD ROLLS

Yield: 100 servings

Ingredients:

    100 French rolls (about 3 inches each)
      1 pound butter
     12 pounds Swiss cheese, cubed
      6 pounds crabmeat or flaked white fish
      1 quart finely diced celery (about 4 pounds)
      3 quarts petite peas, cooked
      2 quarts sour cream
      2 cups chopped parsley
      3 tablespoons seasoned salt
      1 teaspoon white pepper

Cut a thin slice from top of each roll. Pull out insides. Melt the butter, then brush inside of rolls with it.

Combine remaining ingredients in bowl. Then divide and stuff rolls.

Bake at 400 degrees F for 15 minutes or until cheese melts. Garnish with cherry tomatoes and parsley. Serve quickly.

NOTE: Baked Spinach Squares are a nice accompaniment for these sandwiches.

FRESH MUSHROOM-MELT SANDWICHES

Yield: 100 servings

Ingredients:

     34 loaves French bread, thickly cut
      1 pound butter
     15 pounds fresh mushrooms, sliced
      2 pounds butter
      2 tablespoons garlic powder
      2 tablespoons sweet basil
      1 tablespoon granulated onion
      1 tablespoon thyme
         salt and pepper to taste
     10 pounds Monterey Jack cheese (1 1/2-ounce slices)

Butter French bread with first amount of butter. Grill bread until golden brown.

Cook mushrooms in 2 pounds butter with seasonings. Remove mushrooms when done and thicken remaining liquid with a little cornstarch.

Place about 2 ounces of mushrooms per serving on grilled bread. Top with a slice of cheese.

Place in oven at 375 degrees F until cheese melts.

Serve with Tomato and Cucumber Salad dressed with oil and vinegar.

HOT GERMAN TUNA SANDWICHES

Yield: 100 servings

Ingredients:

17	cans (7 ounces each) flaked tuna, drained
2 1/4	gallons shredded cabbage (about 6 1/4 pounds)
2 3/4	cups chopped dill pickles
2/3	cup vinegar
100	hamburger buns
100	slices cheese (about 6 1/2 pounds)

Combine ingredients except buns and cheese. Mix and chill.

Cut rolls in half and spread with butter. Using #16 scoop, place tuna mixture on bottom slice of roll. Top with slice of cheese.

Bake at 400 degrees F for 10 to 12 minutes. Serve 1 tuna portion with 1 toasted top.

TURKEY BLEU

Yield: 100 sandwiches

Ingredients:

2	quarts sour cream
2	quarts mayonnaise
1 1/2	quarts bacon crumbs, crisp
4	pounds bleu cheese, crumbled
3	tablespoons granulated garlic
2	pounds butter, softened
200	slices whole wheat bread
6	quarts shredded lettuce
12	pounds turkey, cooked and thinly sliced
32	avocados, peeled, pitted, thinly sliced, and dipped into lemon juice
1	quart lemon juice
4	cans (16 ounces each) ripe olives, chopped

Combine sour cream through garlic; set aside.

Butter bread; cut 100 slices in half diagonally. Allow 1 whole and 2 half pieces per serving. Arrange bread as in diagram. Dip cut avocado slices in lemon juice and set aside.

Layer 1/4 cup lettuce on bread, then 2 ounces turkey, and a thin layer of avocado slices. Top with 2 ounces of sour cream mixture. Garnish with chopped ripe olives.

Serve with tomato wedges and green pepper rings.

TRIO HOT SANDWICHES

Yield: 100 servings (1 muffin each)

Ingredients:

100	English muffins, split mayonnaise as needed
100	tomato slices
100	cheese slices
10	pounds bacon, fried crisp and crumbled; or sliced salami; or cooked and sliced linguisa

Spread each muffin half with mayonnaise; top with tomato slice, cheese, and meat. Broil until cheese is slightly melted. Serve hot.

7 SALADS, SALAD DRESSINGS, AND SAUCES

SILVER SERVICE

"In a large house there are articles not only of gold and silver, but also of wood and clay; some are for noble purposes and some for ignoble. If a man cleanses himself from the latter, he will be an instrument for noble purposes, made holy, useful to the Master and prepared to do any good work" (2 Timothy 2:20-21).

The women of our church saved Betty Crocker coupons to buy the silverware for its kitchen. We use it for holiday dinners, missionary banquets, and other special events. On these occasions the ladies also bring their silver tea sets and silver serving bowls and platters from home. There are crystal dishes rimmed in gold and linen tablecloths. Everything is polished, sparkling, and clean. That is fitting for the Lord's house.

As vessels of the Lord, we too want to be ready and usable for His highest calling, instruments for noble purposes, prepared to do any good work.

Lord, purify us, shape us, polish us to sterling quality. Make us fit for service on Your banquet table. Amen

By Catherine Lawton

SALADS

CABBAGE AND CARROT SLAW

Yield: 100 servings

Ingredients:

- 10 pounds green cabbage, shredded
- 3 pounds carrots, shredded

Toss together and dress with coleslaw dressing.

Adjust seasoning with sugar, salt, and white pepper.

VARIATION: Add 1 pound thinly sliced or diced green peppers for color.

PEAR AND CREAM CHEESE SALAD

Yield: 104 servings (1 pear half with 1 ounce cream cheese mixture)

Ingredients:

- 3 cans (about 35 halves each) pear halves, chilled and drained
- 6 1/2 pounds cream cheese
  sweet cream
  chopped walnuts (if desired)

Place 8 pear halves, cut side up, on medium platters that have been lined with leaf lettuce or romaine.

Soften cream cheese with equal amount of sweet cream. Place in decorator bag; squeeze 1 ounce cheese mixture into each pear depression. Sprinkle with chopped walnuts.

POTATO SALAD

Yield: 100 servings

Ingredients:

20	pounds potatoes, cooked, peeled, and diced
1/2	gallon (approximately) mayonnaise
1/2	cup grated onion
1 1/2	cups pickle relish
2 1/2	tablespoons sugar
5	tablespoons vinegar
3	tablespoons prepared mustard
1	quart diced celery
1	tablespoon pepper
3/4	cup salt

Mix together all ingredients except potatoes. Gently fold mixture into potatoes.

Garnish with paprika, hard-cooked egg slices, or parsley.

HOT COLESLAW

Yield: 100 servings

Ingredients:

32	pounds cabbage, shredded
6	whole bay leaves
8	whole cloves
2	pounds bacon fat
1	quart stock
1 1/4	cups sugar
3	cups cider vinegar
4	quarts peeled and diced raw apples
9	tablespoons salt
4	teaspoons pepper

Shred cabbage. Put bay leaves and cloves in tea ball or in small gauze bag.

Melt bacon fat and add stock, cabbage, and sugar. Cook 8 minutes. Add vinegar, and cook 5 minutes. Add diced apples, salt, and pepper. Cook 10 more minutes. Remove spice ball and serve.

MANDARIN SALAD

Yield: 104 servings (1 1/2 ounces each)

Ingredients:

      Dressing (below)

1 1/2 No. 10 cans Mandarin oranges, drained
   5 pounds head lettuce, cut (or Romaine)
   1 pound thinly sliced green onions
 26 ounces dressing (below)

DRESSING

10 ounces oil
 8 ounces frozen orange juice concentrate
 4 ounces water
 4 ounces vinegar (Rice wine vinegar gives especially nice flavor.)
 2 teaspoons basil *leaves*

Mix well, and add to Mandarin Salad before serving.

SUGGESTION: Garnish with slivered toasted almonds.

CHICKEN WALNUT SALAD

Yield: 120 servings (6 ounces each)

Ingredients:

 25 pounds cooked white meat of chicken
 15 pounds celery, finely cut
2 1/2 pounds pimiento, cut medium
 10 pounds walnuts, coarsely chopped
  1 quart mayonnaise
  4 tablespoons salt
  1 tablespoon pepper
  1 tablespoon basil
  3 tablespoons lime juice

Toss gently; add enough mayonnaise to make a nice consistency. Season with salt, white pepper, and crushed sweet basil. Sprinkle with a small amount of lime juice.

Serve on lettuce leaves; lightly sprinkle with chopped walnuts.

CRANBERRY SALAD

Yield: 108 servings (2 pans, 13x22x2 inches, cut 6x9, or 4 molds, each 3 quarts)

Ingredients:

    3   pounds strawberry gelatin
    9   cups sugar
    1   gallon plus 1 cup boiling water
    1   gallon plus 1 cup cold water
    9   medium oranges
 4 1/2 pounds raw cranberries
 8 1/2 cups chopped celery
 8 1/2 cups diced apples

Dissolve gelatin and sugar in boiling water. Add cold water.

Grind cranberries and unpeeled seedless oranges. Add to gelatin mixture and chill.

When gelatin begins to thicken, fold in celery and apples.

Chill in molds or rectangular pans until firm. Unmold on lettuce leaves and garnish with mayonnaise if desired.

FRACTURED TACO SALAD

Yield: 100 servings

Ingredients:

 11 1/2 pounds tortilla chips
    10   pounds ground beef
     3   large packages of taco seasoning or to taste
     6   cans (2 1/2 pounds each) refried beans
     3   gallons chopped lettuce
     2   gallons diced tomatoes
     9   pounds medium sharp cheese
         sour cream (if desired)

Following directions on taco seasoning package, brown ground beef until crumbly; add seasoning and water if indicated. On each plate place about 1 1/2 ounces tortilla chips, 2 ounces heated refried beans, and 2 ounces meat mixture. Top with 1/2 cup lettuce, 1/4 cup diced tomatoes, and 1 1/2 ounces shredded cheese.

Garnish with ripe olives and, if desired, a dollop of sour cream.

DO-IT-YOURSELF TACOS: Instead of tortilla chips, allow 2 prepared taco shells per person. Put remaining ingredients into serving bowls, and let guests assemble their own taco.

SALAD BAR FOR 100

Yield: 100 servings (men)

Ingredients:

   1 No. 10 can garbanzo beans
   1 No. 10 can kidney beans
   2 No. 10 cans medium ripe olives, pitted (or 10 No. 300 cans)
   4 pounds croutons
   6 No. 300 cans julienne beets
   5 pounds sliced mushrooms
   3 pounds green peppers, sliced
   3 red cabbages, shredded
  32 heads lettuce
  12 pints cherry tomatoes
   6 bunches broccoli, finely diced
   5 pounds carrots, shredded
   8 sweet onions, sliced
   3 pounds toasted sunflower seeds
  10 pounds cucumbers, sliced
   2 cans (16 ounces each) grated Romano cheese
   2 tins bacon bits

Begin salad bar with a large bowl of mixed leaf lettuces and cabbage. Put other condiments in separate containers. It is desirable to set the table so identical condiments are on both sides of the table; this accommodates 2 lines of diners. End table with grated Romano cheese, sunflower seeds, bacon bits, and large fresh pepper grinder.

If the luncheon is for women, you will have to judge the type of group you are serving. They might eat less salad but have the potential to eat as much as men. It often seems to depend upon the size of the salads the first women in line take; the majority follow suit.

For salad dressings plan on 1 gallon Bleu Cheese, 1 gallon French, and 1 gallon Oil and Vinegar or Herb Dressing (*see* Salad Dressings).

TURKEY OR CHICKEN SALAD DELIGHT

Yield: 105 servings

Ingredients:

9	quarts cooked and cubed poultry
9	quarts finely sliced celery
3 3/4	quarts diced pineapple, drained
4	tablespoons salt
1	tablespoon white pepper
3	cups sliced black olives
6	cups toasted almonds
1	quart mayonnaise
2	tablespoons lemon juice
18	pimientos, diced
105	whole ripe olives

Lightly mix all ingredients up to mayonnaise. Mix mayonnaise with lemon juice; fold into rest of salad. Chill.

Serve on lettuce leaves and garnish each serving with a strip of pimiento, whole almonds, 1 ripe olive, and a dash of paprika or sprig of parsley.

WALDORF SALAD

Yield: 100 servings (1/2 cup each)

Ingredients:

3	quarts diced celery
3	cups mayonnaise
2	cups sour cream
3	tablespoons salt
1 3/4	gallons diced apples, unpeeled (about 8 pounds)
3	cups chopped walnuts
1	cup chopped Maraschino cherries

Combine all ingredients except walnuts and toss well. Add nuts just before serving. If added sooner, they will become soggy.

SALAD DRESSINGS

HERB AND OIL SALAD DRESSING

Yield: about 1 gallon

Ingredients:

- 8 cups oil
- 3 cups wine vinegar
- 3 tablespoons each of marjoram, thyme, and basil
- 1 cup chopped onions
- 1 cup water
- 3 tablespoons salt
- 1 cup chopped parsley

Combine well. Shake again before using.

FAVORITE FRENCH DRESSING

Yield: 1 gallon

Ingredients:

- 1/2 gallon mayonnaise
- 1/2 gallon ketchup
- 2 tablespoons garlic or onion salt
- 1/4 cup Worcestershire sauce
- 1/2 to 1 teaspoon tabasco

Add ketchup slowly to mayonnaise in mixer. Combine with remaining ingredients.

THOUSAND ISLAND DRESSING

Make French Dressing and add 1 quart pickle relish.

LOUIS DRESSING

Yield: 2 quarts

Ingredients:

> 1 pint ketchup
> 1 1/2 quarts mayonnaise
> 1/2 ounce tabasco
> 1 ounce dry mustard
> 2 teaspoons salt
> 1 ounce red pepper
> 1 ounce Worcestershire sauce
> juice from 1 lime

Blend together. Store in refrigerator.

ROQUEFORT OR BLEU CHEESE DRESSING

Yield: 1 1/2 gallons

Ingredients:

> 2 pounds roquefort or bleu cheese
> 1/3 cup anchovy paste
> 1/3 cup chopped chives
> 1/2 gallon mayonnaise
> 1 jar capers, chopped
> 1 1/2 cups lemon juice
> 1/2 gallon sour cream
> 1 1/2 tablespoons salt
> 1 tablespoon pepper
> 3 tablespoons Worcestershire sauce
> 2 teaspoons tabasco

Blend above ingredients except for cheese. Fold in cheese gently. This is an extremely elegant and rich dressing.

SPECIAL SALAD DRESSING

Yield: 3 pints

Ingredients:

    2 eggs
    1 teaspoon dry mustard
    8 ounces oil
    1/2 teaspoon tabasco
    4 lemons, juice only
    2 teaspoons Worcestershire sauce
    1 teaspoon salt
    1 teaspoon white pepper
    4 medium-sized avocados, pitted and peeled
    6 shallot tops
    1 clove garlic
    1 ounce anchovy paste
    8 ounces mayonnaise

Mix together in blender or food processor. Chill at least 2 hours before serving.

SAUCES

BASIC WHITE SAUCE

Yield: enough for 100 servings

Ingredients:

    1 pound butter or margarine (or 2 cups)
    1 pound flour (or 4 cups)
    2 gallons milk, heated
    2 tablespoons salt
    2 teaspoons white pepper

Melt butter; stir in flour until smooth. Add salt and pepper. Add hot milk gradually, stirring constantly. Cook until it is smooth and has just begun to boil (12 to 20 minutes).

MEDIUM WHITE SAUCE

Ingredients:

- 1 1/2 pounds butter (or 3 cups)
- 1 1/2 pounds flour (or 6 cups)
- 2 gallons milk, hot
- 2 tablespoons salt
- 2 teaspoons white pepper

Use Basic White Sauce method.

THICK WHITE SAUCE

Ingredients:

- 2 pounds butter (or 4 cups)
- 2 pounds flour (or 8 cups)
- 2 gallons milk, hot
- 2 tablespoons salt
- 2 teaspoons pepper

Use Basic White Sauce method.

MORNAY SAUCE

Yield: enough for 100 servings

Make Medium White Sauce and add:

- 3 pounds sharp cheddar cheese, grated
- 2 teaspoons Worcestershire sauce
- 1 tablespoon prepared mustard

COWBOY BARBECUE SAUCE

Yield: enough for 100 servings

Ingredients:

- 1 cup vegetable oil
- 2 cups of finely shredded celery, carrots, and garlic that have been cooked in butter*
- 9 cloves garlic
- 4 cups chili sauce
- 1/2 teaspoon dry mustard
- 3 tablespoons brown sugar
- 1 cup honey
- 1 gallon brown sauce
- 1 tablespoon Worcestershire sauce
- 1/3 cup vinegar
- 1/4 cup lemon juice
- salt to taste
- 1 teaspoon cayenne pepper
- 1/2 teaspoon smoke flavor

Combine ingredients and simmer until desired consistency.

*Vegetable soup may be substituted.

RED MEAT MARINADE

Yield: 2 quarts

Ingredients:

- 3 cups soy sauce
- 3 cups sliced green onions
- 1 1/2 cups sherry
- 1 1/2 cups oil
- 3/4 cup red wine vinegar
- 20 cloves garlic, crushed

Mix ingredients together. Marinate steaks or meat 1 hour or more.

Marinade can also be used on whole mushrooms (48) if desired.

TERIYAKI MARINADE: Add 1/4 cup fresh ginger slices and 1 cup sugar or honey.

VIRGINIA'S OWN CIDER SAUCE
FOR APPLE DUMPLINGS OR PUDDING

Yield: 100 servings (1 1/3 ounces each)

Ingredients:

>   2 cans (46 ounces each) apple juice
>   1/4 cup lemon juice
> 1 1/2 cups brown sugar
>   2 cups cold water
>   1 cup butter
>   1/2 cup cornstarch

Mix cornstarch with sugar. Add cold water slowly and stir until smooth. Add to rest of ingredients. Bring to boil slowly, stirring constantly, until it thickens into a clear sauce. Use <u>hot</u>. Do not reheat after refrigeration.

VIRGINIA'S FAMILY RECIPE
FOR 100-YEAR-OLD BOILED CIDER

Cook 1 gallon of fresh cider very slowly (slow cooker is a good way) until it is reduced to 1 pint. Use it for flavoring as you would an extract. It will store for years without refrigeration.

8

BREADS

BREAD IN BIBLE TIMES

According to the prophet Isaiah, bread and water are the "stay and staff" of life (Is. 3:1)—the two essentials without which God's people would perish. . . .

Of the grains grown in the Holy Land, wheat was most commonly used for flour. Whereas barley was sometimes eaten by the poor, it was regularly fed to the domestic animals. Spelt, millet, and even lentils were sometimes ground into flour as an emergency food. . . .

The grinding of flour, as well as the baking of bread, was usually a daily task ("our *daily* bread,"

Matt.6:11) except on the Sabbath day, when, according to the law of Moses, all unnecessary work ceased.

In making the bread, the house wife used flour, yeast, salt, olive oil, and water or milk. She made a thick batter of the flour and liquid, then added the previously soured yeast. The yeast might be made by adding a little sour milk to some flour and letting it stand in a warm place for several hours or overnight. Or a little dough, left from the previous baking, might serve to begin the souring process. The "leaven which a woman took and hid in three measures of meal until the whole was leavened" illustrates the quiet effective working of the Word of God in the hearts of men (Luke 13:21). Only at religious festivals, or when in great haste, did the Israelites eat their bread unleavened (Ex. 12:39, the Passover; Gen. 19:3, Lot). . . . The mixing trough was a deep pan of metal or pottery, its size depending on the amount of dough to be mixed at a time. The consistency of the batter or dough varied according to the type of oven to be used in the baking process.

From *Home Life in Bible Times,* copyright © 1947, 1969 by Concordia Publishing House, pp. 64—70.

WHOLE GRAIN COFFEE CAKE

Yield: 108 servings (2 pans, 18x26x1 inches each, cut 6x9)

Ingredients:

> Topping (below)
> 4 1/4 pounds all-purpose biscuit mix
> 11 ounces rolled oats or wheat
> 8 ounces brown sugar
> 4 teaspoons cinnamon
> 2 7/8 pounds milk (or 5 3/4 cups)
> 16 ounces eggs (about 8 whole)

Combine dry ingredients and mix well. Mix milk and eggs together and add all at once to dry ingredients. Stir only until moistened.

Spread 2 pounds batter in each of the 2 prepared pans; sprinkle with 6 ounces of the topping. Top with remaining batter, and then sprinkle tops with remaining topping.

Bake at 375 degrees F for 35 to 40 minutes, or until cake tests done.

TOPPING

> 14 ounces rolled oats or wheat
> 2 5/8 pounds brown sugar
> 1 pound walnuts, chopped
> 1 pound butter
> 4 teaspoons cinnamon

Mix all ingredients until crumbly.

VIRGINIA'S SOUR CREAM COFFEE CAKE

Ingredients (3 loaf pans):

Topping (below)

3/4	pound butter
3	cups sugar
9	eggs
4 1/2	cups cake flour, sifted
1 1/2	cups all-purpose flour
1	tablespoon soda
1	tablespoon baking powder
1 1/4	pounds sour cream
1	tablespoon vanilla

TOPPING

3	cups packed brown sugar
1/2	pound butter, chilled
1	cup cake flour
1	teaspoon cinnamon
1	teaspoon salt
3	cups nuts

Ingredients (1 pan, 18x26x1 inches, cut 8x10, or 13x22x1-1/2 inches, cut 6x9):

Topping (below)

1	pound butter
4	cups sugar
12	eggs
6	cups cake flour, sifted
2	cups all-purpose flour
4	teaspoons soda
4	teaspoons baking powder
2	pounds sour cream
4	teaspoons vanilla

TOPPING

3	cups packed brown sugar
1/2	pound butter, chilled
1	cup cake flour
1	teaspoon cinnamon
1	teaspoon salt
3	cups nuts

Ingredients (large loaf pans, cut 12):

> Topping (below)

1 1/2	pounds butter
6	cups sugar
18	eggs
9	cups cake flour, sifted
3	cups all-purpose flour
2	tablespoons soda
2	tablespoons baking powder
2 1/2	pounds sour cream
2	tablespoons vanilla

TOPPING

4 1/2	cups packed brown sugar
3/4	pound butter, chilled
1 1/2	cups cake flour
1 1/2	teaspoons cinnamon
1 1/2	teaspoons salt
4 1/2	cups nuts

Mix topping ingredients together until uniformly crumbly. Set aside.

Cream butter and sugar thoroughly. Add eggs and beat well. Mix together dry ingredients. Add to egg batter alternately with sour cream and vanilla.

Spread in pans using half batter, half topping, remaining batter, and final topping of crumbs. Bake at 350 degrees F for 30 minutes.

HOT CAKES

Yield: 100 servings (2 cakes per person; 1/2 cup batter per cake)

Ingredients:

11	pounds flour (or 2 3/4 gallons)
2	cups sugar (or 1 pound)
2/3	cup baking powder
2	tablespoons salt
2	gallons whole milk (or 1 gallon each of water and evaporated milk mixed together)
2 3/4	cups melted shortening or oil

Mix first 5 ingredients together until smooth. Stir in melted shortening or oil.

MIDWESTERN COFFEE CAKE

Yield: 100 servings

Ingredients:

- 1 1/2 quarts brown sugar
- 1 1/2 quarts white sugar
- 1 1/2 quarts butter
- 2 3/4 quarts flour
- 2 1/4 quarts rolled wheat (Pettijohns)
- 12 eggs, beaten
- 1 1/2 quarts buttermilk
- 2 tablespoons soda
- 1 1/2 teaspoons salt
- 1 1/2 quarts chopped raisins, prunes, dates, figs, apples or apricots

Mix sugar with butter. Add flour and rolled wheat and mix until crumbly. Set aside 6 cups for topping.

Add eggs to original batch. Stir soda and salt into buttermilk and add to dry ingredients. Beat until smooth. Pour into 2 prepared 18x26x1-inch bun pans.

Combine reserved crumbs and dried fruit. Sprinkle over batter.

Bake at 350 degrees F for 30 minutes. When cool, drizzle with glaze made from sifted confectioners' sugar and strong hot coffee.

OATMEAL MUFFINS

Yield: 150

Ingredients:

- 10 cups rolled quick oats or wheat
- 10 cups buttermilk
- 10 large eggs, beaten
- 5 cups packed brown sugar
- 10 cups flour
- 3 1/2 tablespoons baking powder
- 2 tablespoons plus 2 teaspoons salt
- 1 tablespoon plus 2 teaspoons soda
- 1 pound plus 11 ounces shortening, melted (or 3 1/3 cups)

Soak rolled grain in buttermilk until liquid is absorbed. Set aside. Measure dry ingredients together. Lightly beat eggs and add to buttermilk mixture. Add dry ingredients to liquid ingredients all at once. Blend only until moistened; do not overmix.

Use a #24 scoop to portion batter into paper muffin tins.

Bake at 400 degrees F for 20 minutes.

RAISIN MUFFINS

Yield: 100

Ingredients:

6	ounces compressed yeast
2	cups lukewarm water
1 1/2	cups sugar
3	tablespoons salt
1	cup butter
2	cups hot water
2	cans (13 ounces each) evaporated milk
10	eggs
5	quarts flour, sifted
1	quart raisins

Mix yeast with lukewarm water and pinch of sugar; set aside for 5 minutes.

Mix sugar, salt, and butter with hot water. Add evaporated milk, eggs, yeast mixture, and about half the flour. Beat well to blend. Add remaining flour and raisins; beat until smooth. Let rise in warm place until doubled in volume, about 2 hours.

Stir dough and fill greased muffin tins 2/3 full. Let rise until doubled, about 1 hour.

Bake at 375 degrees F for 12 to 15 minutes.

WHOLE GRAIN MUFFINS

Yield: 108 muffins

Ingredients:

- 7 1/2 cups Quaker unprocessed bran or bran cereal
- 7 1/2 cups milk
- 10 eggs, beaten
- 2 1/2 cups vegetable oil
- 2 1/2 cups honey or molasses
- 1 1/4 cups brown sugar
- 2 1/2 quarts Quaker oats, uncooked
- 6 2/3 cups flour
- 2/3 cup baking powder
- 2 1/2 teaspoons salt
- 1 quart raisins, chopped dry fruit, nuts, or apples

Combine milk and bran cereal; add eggs, oil, molasses, and brown sugar. Mix well and set aside.

Mix together remaining dry ingredients. Add to bran mixture and stir only until dry ingredients are just moistened. Do not overmix.

With #20 scoop, fill paper-lined muffin pans.

Bake 400 degrees F for 15 to 18 minutes or until muffins are lightly browned and test done.

VIRGINIA'S 100-YEAR-OLD FAMILY RECIPE FOR SHORTCAKE BISCUITS

Yield: 200 medium

Ingredients:

- 2 gallons flour
- 1 cup plus 5 tablespoons baking powder
- 2 1/2 tablespoons salt
- 4 cups sugar
- 5 1/3 cups shortening
- 16 eggs
- 5 1/3 cups milk

Blend together first 4 ingredients; then cut in shortening.

In separate bowl beat eggs with milk. Add to flour-shortening mixture.

Roll out dough to about a 3/4-inch thickness. Cut into shape. Prick with fork. Bake at 375 degrees F for 15 minutes.

SCONES: Add currants or raisins to shortcake biscuits.

DELICIOUS BANANA BREAD

Yield: 100 slices

Ingredients:

- 3 cups shortening
- 3 cups white sugar
- 3 cups packed brown sugar
- 2 quarts mashed bananas
- 1/2 cup lemon juice
- 1 gallon flour, sifted
- 5 tablespoons baking powder
- 1 1/2 tablespoons salt
- 1 1/2 tablespoons baking soda
- 13 eggs
- 3 cups milk
- 2 cups walnuts or pecans
- 2 cups coconut, toasted

Cream shortening with white and brown sugar until fluffy. Add mashed bananas and lemon juice. Sift together dry ingredients. Beat eggs and milk together. Alternating between dry and wet ingredients, gradually add them to the shortening-sugar mixture. Mix well. Add nuts and coconut.

Put about 2 pounds of mixture each into loaf pans measuring 9x5x2 3/4 inches.

Bake at 350 degrees F for about 1 hour or until bread tests done. Leave bread in pans 10 minutes before turning out to cool.

Bread is best if allowed to rest at least 12 hours before slicing.

SCOTCH SCONES

Yield: 100

Ingredients:

   3 3/4 quarts quick oats, uncooked
   5 pounds flour
   3/4 cup baking powder
   1 cup cream of tartar
   1 1/2 tablespoons salt
   3 cups sugar
   4 pounds margarine, melted
   1 quart milk
   12 eggs
   6 cups raisins (or 2 pounds, 4 ounces)

Combine first 6 ingredients, mixing well. Set aside.

Combine butter, milk and eggs; add to dry ingredients, and mix just until moistened. Do not overmix. Stir in raisins.

Divide into 12 balls about 1 pound, 9 1/2 ounces each. Roll into 8-inch circles. Cut each circle into 8 to 10 wedges.

Bake at 425 degrees F for 14 to 16 minutes or until lightly browned. Serve warm.

VIRGINIA'S BONA FIDE JOHNNY CAKE (CORNBREAD)

Yield: 80 servings

Ingredients:

   18 ounces shortening
   3 cups sugar
   6 eggs
   6 cups cornmeal
   6 cups flour
   2 1/4 tablespoons salt
   2 1/4 tablespoons soda
   6 cups buttermilk or sour milk*

Cream shortening, sugar, and eggs until fluffy.

Mix dry ingredients together and add to egg mixture, alternately with buttermilk. Mix only until blended. Do not overmix. Begin and end with the dry ingredients.

Using a scale, place about 1/2 pound of batter into each of 10 prepared pie pans. Bake at 350 degrees F for 25 to 30 minutes or until cakes test done. Cut each cake into 8 wedges.

To sour fresh milk, use 1 tablespoon or 1/2 ounce vinegar for each cup of sour milk desired plus enough sweet milk to make 1 cup. Allow mixture to stand until chemical reaction has time to complete process (a few minutes).

FRECKLED ROLLS

Yield: 100 rolls

Ingredients:

>   3 cups uncooked bulgur
>   1 quart hot water
>   3/4 cup dry yeast
>   2 cups lukewarm water
>   1 3/4 cups margarine
>   2 1/2 cups nonfat dry milk
>   1 3/4 cups sugar
>   1/2 cup salt
> 8 to 8 1/2 quarts flour

Soak bulgur in hot water overnight or at least 1 hour.

Combine yeast and lukewarm water with pinch of sugar. Set aside. Mix to gether margarine, milk, sugar, and salt; add dissolved yeast mixture and half of the flour. Blend well. Slowly add bulgur and rest of flour until dough is a smooth consistency and will leave side of bowl in a soft ball.

Set dough in warm place to rise until double in bulk, about 2 hours. Punch down and form into desired shape; place on prepared baking sheet. Let rise until doubled. Bake at 400 degrees F for 12 to 15 minutes or until brown.

POPOVERS

Yield: 150

Ingredients:

     1 1/2 gallons milk
     1 1/2 cups butter, melted
     1 1/2 gallons flour, sifted
         2 tablespoons salt
        50 eggs (or 8 1/3 cups)

Mix together just until smooth. Pour muffin tins 3/4 full.

Preheat oven to 450 degrees F. Place popovers in oven, and bake 15 minutes. Then without opening oven, lower temperature to 350 degrees F and continue baking for 20 minutes.

Either serve immediately or prick each muffin with a skewer to let steam escape and then let them sit in the oven with door ajar for 5 minutes. This will dry out inside of popovers.

9 EGGS, CHEESE, RICE, AND PASTA

RECIPE FOR A HOME

Take a half a cup of friendship;
Add a cup of thoughtfulness;
Cream together with a
Pinch of powdered tenderness.
Very lightly beat in
A bowl of loyalty
With a cup of faith, one of hope
And one of charity.

Be sure to add a spoonful each
Of gaiety that sings
And also the ability to laugh
At little things.
Moisten with the sudden tears
Of heartfelt sympathy.
Bake in a good-natured pan
And serve repeatedly.

Author unknown

EGGS AND CHEESE

CALICO CUTS

Yield: 25 servings, cut 4x6 inches or 208 appetizers, cut 1-1/2x2 inches

Ingredients:

    20 eggs
     2 quarts evaporated milk
     3 tablespoons salt
     3 tablespoons celery seed
 2 1/2 cups chopped pimiento
    10 pounds cheese, shredded
 1 1/2 tablespoons black pepper
       Bisquick mix

Beat eggs; add remaining ingredients.

Roll out a thin crust from Bisquick mix and place it in a pan measuring 26x17 inches. Pour egg mixture on top of this. Bake for 12 to 15 minutes at 375 degrees F.

This makes a good appetizer.

Eggs,
Cheese,
Rice,
and
Pasta

100

SCRAMBLED EGGS

Yield: 100 servings

Ingredients:

    2 gallons beaten eggs
    1 quart milk or water
       salt and pepper to taste

Water tends to keep eggs from separating as they sit.

PROFESSIONAL TIP: To prepare scrambled eggs successfully for a crowd, steam eggs, rather than cooking on top of stove. Here are some ways of doing this:

1. Use very large double boiler.
2. Use a baking pan set into larger pan of boiling water. Cover and bake at 325 degrees F for about 1 hour.
3. Bake, covered, without water bath if you have exceptionally good baking pans (even heat diffusion).

As eggs cook, they should be gently stirred about every 10 minutes.

HOT CHICKEN STRATA

Yield: 100 servings

Ingredients:

      2 pounds butter
    2/3 cup prepared mustard
      4 pounds sharp cheddar cheese, shredded (reserve 1 pound for topping)
     11 pounds chicken, cooked and diced
     10 pounds frozen peas, cooked
      1 quart chopped onions
      1 pint chopped pimiento
  1 1/2 tablespoons salt
  1 1/2 teaspoons pepper
      1 pound butter
      5 quarts condensed cream of chicken soup
     64 eggs, beaten
      6 quarts milk
    200 slices white bread

Soften first amount of butter and beat together with mustard. Use to spread on white bread. Trim off crusts.

Arrange half of bread slices in greased baking pans with buttered side up. Combine cheese, chicken, peas, onions, and pimiento with salt and pepper; spread over bread. Cover with other slice of bread, buttering exposed sides.

Blend soup, eggs, and milk. Pour over sandwiches in pan. Sprinkle with reserved cheese and bake at 325 degrees F for 30 minutes or until golden brown.

Serve with cranberry jelly and cabbage slaw.

Eggs,
Cheese,
Rice,
and
Pasta

101

QUICHE LORRAINE

Yield: 100 servings (13 pies, 10 inches each, or 100 individual pies, 4 1/2 inches each)

Ingredients:

- 3/4 pound onions, sliced or diced
- 12 ounces margarine
- 3 1/2 pounds bacon, diced and cooked crisp
    pastry shells
- 7 pounds eggs, beaten
- 11 pounds Swiss cheese, shredded
- 7 quarts milk
- 1 3/4 cups flour
- 2 tablespoons salt
- 2 teaspoons nutmeg
- 1/2 teaspoon cayenne pepper

Cook onions in margarine until limp. Toss with crisp-fried bacon. Sprinkle on pie shells.

Mix flour with cheese and seasonings. Add eggs and milk. Pour mixture into pie shells.

Bake 30 minutes at 350 degrees F.

MEXICAN QUICHE: Omit bacon and nutmeg. Add 2 packages taco seasoning and use cheddar cheese in place of Swiss. Add 2 cups chopped green peppers.

SPINACH QUICHE: Add 6 packages (10 ounces each) frozen, chopped, cooked, well-drained spinach. (Omit bacon, if desired.) Dust top with Parmesan cheese.

Eggs,
Cheese,
Rice,
and
Pasta

102

CHEESE SOUFFLÉ A-1

Yield: 90 servings (4 ounces each)

Ingredients:

3	cups butter
4 1/2	cups flour
1 1/2	cups water
4 1/2	cups nonfat dry milk
3/4	teaspoon white pepper
3/4	teaspoon nutmeg
6	tablespoons prepared mustard
12	drops tabasco
8	teaspoons salt
3	pounds cheddar cheese, shredded
45	eggs

Melt butter; blend in flour, and cook until mixture bubbles. Add water and dry milk, and continue cooking until thick and smooth, stirring constantly. Add seasonings.

Remove from heat. Blend in cheese; cool slightly.

Separate eggs. Beat yolks until thick; stir into sauce.

Beat egg whites until stiff; fold into sauce carefully.

Turn into counter pans. Bake at 300 degrees F for 1 1/2 hours or until lightly set in center.

This soufflé requires a long, slow cooking. It is firm enough to retain its shape throughout the serving period.

VIRGINIA'S VERY BEST CHEESE SOUFFLÉ

Yield: 144 servings

Ingredients:

1 1/2	gallons milk
40	ounces quick tapioca
1 1/2	gallons cheddar cheese
8	dozen eggs, separated
8	teaspoons cream of tartar
8	teaspoons salt

Combine milk and tapioca, and let stand 10 minutes.

Cook milk and tapioca over medium heat, stirring constantly until very thick (about 5 minutes after boil). Add cheese and stir until melted. Remove from heat.

Beat egg yolks until thick; add slowly to milk mixture.

Combine egg whites, cream of tartar, and salt. Beat at high speed until stiff but not dry. Pour cheese mixture over white mixture and mix at very low speed until just combined (about 30 seconds).

Turn into 3 prepared shallow hotel pans.

Bake at 325 degrees F for 55 to 65 minutes.

Eggs,
Cheese,
Rice,
and
Pasta

103

____RICE____

Rice may be prepared by two methods: boiling-steaming or pilaf.

BOIL OR STEAM METHOD: Use 2 1/3 to 3 parts water to 1 part rice by volume. Gradually stir rice into boiling, salted water. Cover pot and lower heat to barely simmering. Cook until tender, at least 20 minutes. When rice is tender, drain excess water that has not been absorbed.

PILAF METHOD: Use approximately 2 parts water or stock to 1 part rice by volume. Stir-fry rice in small amount of butter, margarine, or other fat until all grains are well coated.

Add boiling water or stock in correct proportion to rice. Add stir-fried green, yellow, or red onion and any combination of herbs desired, for example, parsley, savory, and thyme. Cover pot. Complete cooking over low heat or in oven at 200 degrees F. Rice will be light and fluffy when done.

Requires 1 hour cooking in oven at 200 degrees F; 20 minutes at 375 degrees F.

AMERICAN STEAMED RICE

Yield: 104 servings

Ingredients:

    4 1/2 quarts dry rice
       2   gallons water
       1   tablespoon salt

Mix ingredients together and steam approximately 40 to 60 minutes in a 4-to 4 1/2-inch deep hotel pan.

ORANGE, MUSHROOM, PECAN RICE

Yield: 104 servings

Ingredients:

    1   gallon plus 1 1/2 cups rice
    1   pound margarine, melted
    1   pound celery, finely chopped
    8   ounces onion, finely chopped
    1   gallon chicken broth
    1   quart frozen orange juice concentrate
    1   quart sherry
    2   tablespoons whole rosemary
    3   tablespoons sugar
    3   pounds mushrooms, washed and sliced, stir-fried in margarine
   12   ounces pecans, toasted and chopped

Mix chicken broth and frozen orange juice concentrate together. Combine all ingredients except mushrooms and pecans, and steam 45 minutes or until all liquid is absorbed.

Just before serving, stir mushrooms and pecans into rice with a large fork.

RICE PILAF

Eggs,
Cheese,
Rice,
and
Pasta

105

Yield: 3 gallons (about 100 servings)

Ingredients:

- 5 cups mushrooms, sliced
- 9 ounces margarine or fat
- 21 ounces onions, finely diced
- 4 1/2 ounces salt
- 3/4 teaspoon white pepper
- 2 1/2 gallons chicken stock
- 7 pounds plus 3 ounces uncooked rice
- 1 cup chopped parsley

Cook mushrooms in margarine; add onions and seasoning. Bake rice at 400 degrees F until evenly browned.

Bring stock to a boil; add rice and remaining ingredients. Cover and put in oven for 45 minutes. Prior to serving, stir rice with fork to distribute the mushrooms and onions. Garnish with parsley.

PASTA

Yield: Generally 1 pound of pasta boiled in 3 to 4 quarts of water yields 3 pounds of cooked pasta.

To cook pasta, use 4 parts boiling salted water to 1 part pasta. Adding a light layer of oil to the surface of boiling water prior to adding pasta will help to keep the noodles from sticking together. Do not stir until the pasta has been added to the pot. Then stir to separate strands and keep them from sticking to the bottom. Do not cover the pot.

Cooking times vary according to the product. The following are general lengths of time for the products indicated:

Macaroni	15 to 20 minutes
Noodles	8 to 10 minutes
Spaghetti	15 to 20 minutes

10 MEATS

UNEXPECTED GUESTS

"When Jesus looked up and saw a great crowd coming toward him, he said to Philip, 'Where shall we buy bread for these people to eat?' He asked this only to test him, for he already had in mind what he was going to do.

"Philip answered him, 'Eight months' wages would not buy enough bread for each one to have a bite!'

"Another of his disciples, Andrew, Simon Peter's brother, spoke up, 'Here is a boy with five small barley loaves and two small fish, but how far will they go among so many?'

"Jesus said, 'Have the people sit down.' There was plenty of grass in that place, and the men sat down, about five thousand of them. Jesus then took the loaves, gave thanks, and distributed to those who were seated as much as they wanted. He did the same with the fish.

"When they had all had enough to eat, he said to his disciples, 'Gather the pieces that are left over. Let nothing be wasted.' So they gathered them and filled twelve baskets with the pieces of the five barley loaves left over by those who had eaten" (John 6:5-13).

Dear Jesus, there are more people at the banquet tonight than I expected. So many mouths to feed. Thank You that You know how I feel.

Help me to face this emergency with the same calm and order You exemplified when You had 5,000 hungry people to feed. (And thank You that I don't have that many, even if it does seem like it!)

Help me to use what I have at hand as You did, trusting the Father to meet every need.

And most of all, thank You for being with me. Amen

By Donna Crow

____ABOUT MEAT____

As meat thaws, a large quantity of juice, which is part of the cost of the meat, is lost. Consequently, cooking meat while it is still frozen and in its own juice is economically advantageous. It also results in a better finished product. Meat at room temperature cooks more rapidly when subjected to heat than does chilled meat. Cooking time for frozen meat is 2 to 3 times that of refrigerated meat. As the cooking temperature increases, time is decreased; but high temperatures also increase shrinkage and reduce the appearance, juiciness, tenderness, and flavor of the meat.

Bone-in-meat conducts heat faster than meat alone. As a result, a cut of meat with a bone will cook faster. Insert the meat thermometer in the center of the meat section. If the thermometer is placed next to the bone, it will register higher than the true meat temperature actually is.

Large pieces of meat continue to increase in internal temperature even after being removed from the heat source. If you want a rare or medium roast, remove it from its heat source when the temperature on the meat thermometer reads 15 to 25 degrees lower than the desired finished internal temperature.

Allowing meat to rest for about 30 minutes prior to carving is desirable. This means letting the meat stand outside its cooking environment. During this time the heat pressure is released, allowing the juices to distribute more evenly and the meat to firm up.

Meats

When slicing meat, quarter a large piece of meat first to determine the direction of the grain. Cut meat across the grain. This shortens the long, stringy, tough fibers, making the meat more tender to chew.

The cost of meat is the most expensive item on your menu, so carefully consider the size of each portion. Allow only 1 portion per person. A scale is helpful for maintaining uniformity of serving size.

BEEF

TENDERLOIN TIPS IN MUSHROOM SAUCE

Yield: 100 servings

Ingredients:

    34 pounds tenderloin tips
     6 pounds mushrooms, sliced
     2 pounds shallots, chopped
     6 ounces butter
     3 gallons cooked brown sauce, hot
    12 ounces Burgundy
     2 pints salad oil
     2 tablespoons Worcestershire sauce

Slice meat on the bias. Cook shallots and mushrooms in butter until tender. Add brown sauce, wine, and salt and pepper to taste. Simmer this slowly, while preparing meat.

Heat salad oil until hot; add meat and fry quickly until nicely brown.

Add meat to mushrooms, then Worcestershire sauce, and bring to slow boil. Serve.

This may be served in small casseroles or thickened slightly and served on a plate.

SUGGESTION: Garnish by dipping small toast points in melted butter and then into chopped parsley. Stick toast points deep into side of casserole.

BEST-EVER BAKED SWISS STEAK

Yield: 104 servings

Ingredients:

- 104 portions steaks, cube beef
- 2 quarts flour
- 2 tablespoons seasoned salt
- 1 teaspoon thyme
- 1 teaspoon marjoram
- 1 teaspoon basil
- 1 quart chopped onions

Brown both sides of steaks on grill. Arrange in baking pan so that steaks overlap.

Make 1 gallon of gravy out of meat drippings and beef roux. When gravy is consistency of honey, add seasonings, and taste for adjustment. Pour gravy over steaks and scatter onions on top. Cover tightly and bake at 325 degrees F for 2 hours.

BARBECUE BEEF—COUNTRY STYLE

Yield: 100 servings

Ingredients:

- 38 1/4 pounds brisket of beef
- 3 cups diced onion
- 17 small carrots, diced
- 9 cups diced celery
- 9 garlic cloves, crushed
- 9 cups water
- salt and pepper to taste
- 20 bay leaves

Combine all ingredients in one roasting pan. Roast at 350 degrees F for 2 hours.

After 2 hours test for doneness. If meat is not tender, add more water and turn. Continue testing frequently until meat is fork tender.

BRAISED SHORT RIBS WITH ZIPPY SAUCE

Yield: 100 servings (10 ounces each)

Ingredients:

  100 short ribs (10 ounces each)
        flour
    3 pounds onions, cut into eighths
    1 pound carrots, cut into 1-inch slices
    1 pound celery, cut into 1-inch slices
    1 quart salad oil
    4 teaspoons sweet basil
    1 teaspoon thyme
    6 quarts hot beef stock
    6 quarts beer
    1 tablespoon tabasco
  1/2 No. 10 can ketchup
    1 pint molasses
    1 pint vinegar
    1 tablespoon salt

Roll ribs in flour. Shake off excess. Brown in oil and put into roasting pan. Combine remaining ingredients. Cover and simmer for 2 1/2 hours or until meat is tender.

SWEDISH MEATBALLS

Yield: 125 servings (2 meatballs each)

Ingredients:

    30 eggs
 1 1/4 quarts milk
     5 quarts bread crumbs
    25 pounds ground pork
    25 pounds ground beef
    25 pounds ground veal
     1 quart finely diced celery
     1 quart chopped onions
     1 cup salt
     2 tablespoons pepper

Beat eggs. Add milk and bread crumbs; let mixture stand until moisture is absorbed. Add remaining ingredients in order given; mix well.

Using a #16 scoop, form meat into balls. Roll in flour and place on baking pans. Bake at 425 degrees F until browned. Remove meatballs, and make gravy if desired. Return meatballs to the oven at 350 degrees F, and cook 1 hour more.

Meats

VIRGINIA'S MEAT LOAF

Yield: 100 servings

Ingredients:

    25   pounds ground beef
  2 1/2 quarts fine bread crumbs or oats
     1   quart brewed coffee
  1 1/2 quarts evaporated milk
    12   eggs
     4   onions, chopped fine
     1   bunch celery, chopped fine
     1   bunch parsley, chopped fine
   1/2   cup dry beef base
     2   tablespoons salt
     2   teaspoons pepper
     1   tablespoon marjoram
     1   tablespoon thyme
     2   tablespoons garlic
     2   tablespoons poultry seasoning
     2   tablespoons monosodium glutamate (MSG)

Mix all ingredients except meat in a large bowl, using a dough hook or hands. Allow crumbs to absorb moisture. By hand, gently mix in meat just until blended. Do not overmix!

Form 3 loaves and place in baking pans. Bake at 350 degrees F for 1 to 1 1/2 hours or until done.

PIGGY BEEF BAKE

Yield: 100 servings

Ingredients:

        4 pounds fine noodles, uncooked
        2 cups margarine
        2 gallons cooked beef or pork
        3 No. 5 cans condensed cream of chicken soup
    1 1/2 No. 10 cans vacuumed-packed whole kernel corn, undrained
        2 gallons shredded cheese
       17 green peppers, finely chopped
        2 cans pimiento

Cook noodles. Drain. Melt margarine and brown meat. Drain off fat. Stir in noodles, soup, corn with liquid, pimiento, cheese, and green peppers.

Pour into casseroles.

Bake uncovered at 375 degrees F for 45 minutes.

ORIENTAL BEEF AND PEPPERS
(CHINESE PEPPER STEAK)

Yield: 100 servings

Ingredients:

       32 pounds beef tenderloin, thinly sliced
       25 cups au jus or beef stock
       25 cups onion soup
    12 1/2 cups canned mushrooms, drained
    12 1/2 cups Burgundy wine
        2 tablespoons salt or to taste
        1 teaspoon pepper
      1/4 cup soy sauce
        1 tablespoon freshly ground ginger
     8 1/2 tablespoons cornstarch
       66 tomatoes, each cut in six wedges
       40 green peppers, cut in tenths
        1 No. 10 can water chestnuts, sliced

Stir-fry slices of meat in pan. Remove meat and keep warm.

In same pan as meat was cooked, add broth, onion soup, mushrooms, wine, salt, pepper, ginger, and soy sauce. Simmer to light boil. Mix cornstarch with enough water to make thin consistency. Thicken simmering broth with this mixture. Add stir-fried meat and remaining ingredients to sauce.

Serve with white rice.

OLD WORLD CORNISH PASTRY

Yield: 100 pastries

Ingredients:

> Pastry for 20 circles (9 inches each) (below)

20	pounds beef (chili ground steak)
1	gallon scrubbed, raw-ground potatoes
6	cups chopped parsley
2 to 2 1/2	quarts chopped onions
8	tablespoons salt
2	tablespoons pepper

Mix well. Using a 1-cup measure, portion 1 cup filling (not packed) onto a pastry circle. Dot with butter or margarine. Fold pastry in half and crimp edges together.

Bake at 350 degrees F for 1 hour.

PASTRY

14	cups flour
4	cups Crisco
5	teaspoons salt
	water

Mix well in large tub. Add about 4 cups cold water or until pastry is right consistency.

From Dorothy Peavy

CHILI CON CARNE

Yield: 100 servings

Ingredients:

- 1 cup fat or oil
- 16 pounds ground beef
- 3 cups chopped onions
- 2 tablespoons minced garlic (optional)
- 2 1/2 quarts uncooked bulgur
- 1/3 cup chili powder
- 1/4 cup salt
- 2 teaspoons pepper
- 1 tablespoon powdered cumin
- 1 tablespoon oregano
- 2 gallons beef stock
- 2 quarts tomato puree
- 1 No. 10 can spiced western beans*

Heat oil; add beef, onions, garlic, and bulgur. Cook until brown. Add seasonings, then remaining ingredients. Place in 4 baking pans (20x12x2 inches each). Cover tightly with foil. Bake at 350 degrees F for 1 1/2 to 2 hours.

Serve with generous topping of grated cheddar cheese and/or green onions.

Pinto beans can be substituted (adjust seasoning with chili powder).

LAMB

FRENCH LAMB

Yield: 100 servings

Ingredients:

     25 1/2 pounds lamb, leg or shoulder
          8 pounds bacon, chopped
         17 onions, chopped
         17 cloves garlic
         17 medium carrots, cut in chunks
          1 cup tomato puree
      1 1/2 gallons button mushrooms
          1 gallon red wine
             salt and pepper to taste
        1/2 cup sugar
          1 cup flour
          1 cup chopped parsley

Fry bacon in large deep pan until crisp. Drain. Add onion and garlic to bacon drippings and fry until brown. Cube lamb and add to onions; add carrots. Brown on all sides. Return bacon to pan with mushrooms, tomato puree, wine, seasonings, and sugar, and bring to boil.

Bake at 350 degrees F for 1 1/2 hours.

Thicken meat drippings in pan with flour that has been mixed with water to a smooth creamy consistency.

Garnish with chopped parsley.

___PORK___

SESAME DRESSING FOR PORK OR POULTRY

Yield: 100 servings (using #24 scoop)

Ingredients:

      1 1/2 quarts chicken broth
      2 quarts chopped celery
      4 quarts 1/2-inch bread cubes
      1 quart chopped onions
      2 cups margarine
      2 cups sesame seeds, toasted
      8 tablespoons poultry seasoning
     16 eggs, beaten slightly
         salt and pepper to taste

Cook onions and celery in margarine. Toss with remaining ingredients. Use a #24 scoop per serving to stuff pork chops, or put 2 pork chops together with dressing in between them like a sandwich and bake at 350 degrees F for 1 1/2 hours.

HUNGARIAN PORK—HUNTER STYLE

Yield: 100 servings

Ingredients:

     24 pounds lean pork, cut into 1-inch cubes
     32 ounces oil
      6 pounds onions, sliced
      4 No. 10 cans sauerkraut
      2 cups paprika
      2 cups dry white wine
      5 bay leaves
      6 whole cloves
    1/2 teaspoon crushed thyme
      2 gallons beef stock

Cook meat in oil until browned. Dust meat with flour; brown in oven at 200 degrees F for 10 minutes.

To the oil that the meat was browned in, add onions, and cook until browned. Add to meat. Combine remaining ingredients and add to meat and onions in large casserole. Simmer slowly for 2 hours. Taste and season with salt and pepper.

Serve with buttered noodles.

PORK CHOW MEIN

Yield: 104 servings

Ingredients:

- 12 pounds celery, cut diagonally
- 1 quart oil
- 12 pounds onions, cut diagonally
- 4 tablespoons monosodium glutamate (MSG)
- 13 pounds raw pork, cubed
- 1 No. 10 can water chestnuts, drained and sliced (reserve juice)
- 2 No. 10 cans bean sprouts, drained (reserve juice)
- 2 pounds cornstarch
- 1 quart cold water
- 1 quart soy sauce
- 3 cups canned or fresh red peppers or diced green peppers

Cook celery in oil for 5 minutes. Add onions and MSG, and cook another 7 to 8 minutes. Set aside.

Brown pork cubes in oven. Add 2 gallons of liquid (use reserved liquids from above canned goods plus water to make amount needed). Continue to bake pork until tender. Add water chestnuts, bean sprouts, celery mixture, and peppers.

Mix cornstarch with cold water and soy sauce. Add to above meat and vegetables and continue cooking, stirring often, until clear and thickened. If too thick, add chicken stock until it is right consistency.

Serve over fluffy steamed rice, and garnish with crisp noodles and buttered frozen or fresh green peas.

HAM LOAF

Yield: 125 servings

Ingredients:

> 15 pounds ground pork
> 15 pounds smoked ham, ground
>   3 quarts cracker crumbs
> 1 1/3 tablespoons salt
>   3/4 teaspoon pepper
> 20 eggs, beaten
> 1 1/4 quarts pineapple juice
> 1 1/4 No. 10 cans crushed pineapple

Mix meats together; add cracker crumbs, salt, and pepper. Combine slightly beaten eggs with juice, and add to meat mixture. Blend thoroughly.

Place 5 pounds meat mixture into each loaf pan. Top each pan with crushed pineapple.

Bake in oven at 325 degrees F for 3 hours.

ALTERNATE: Tomato soup, or puree, or canned tomatoes can be used in place of pineapple. Substitute juice with milk.

CORN AND FRANK ESCALLOP

Yield: 100 servings

Ingredients:

>   1 quart chopped onions
>   2 cups chopped green peppers
> 1/2 cup margarine, melted
> 100 all meat frankfurters, cut up (about 12 pounds, 8 ounces)
>   3 No. 10 cans cream style corn
> 3 3/4 quarts whole kernel corn, drained
>   4 teaspoons salt
>   1 teaspoon pepper
>   2 tablespoons Worcestershire sauce
>   2 quarts grated sharp cheddar cheese
>   1 quart cracker crumbs

Cook onions in margarine. Combine remaining ingredients except for cheese and crackers. Place in 2 baking pans, each measuring 12x20x2 inches. Sprinkle with cheese, then with cracker crumbs.

Bake at 375 degrees F for 40 minutes.

VEAL

VEAL PARMESAN

Yield: 100 servings

Ingredients:

- 100 portions (5 1/4 ounces each) veal steak or veal cubed steak
- 3 gallons fine bread crumbs
- 1 tablespoon crushed oregano
- 1/2 cup chicken base
- 2 tablespoons white pepper
- 1/2 cup chopped dry parsley
- 1 quart grated Parmesan cheese
- 1 gallon buttermilk
- 1 gallon milk
- 100 slices mozzarella cheese

Mix together ingredients from bread crumbs to Parmesan cheese. Combine buttermilk and milk, and dip meat portion into this mixture. Place on baking tray. Bake at 325 degrees F for 40 minutes.

Remove meat from oven, and place a slice of mozzarella cheese on top of each portion. Allow cheese to melt by either placing meat under broiler for a minute or by returning it to oven. Watch it carefully so that cheese does not completely melt and run off the meat.

Heat 1 No. 10 can of spaghetti sauce. Place 1 cup of sauce on each platter and 8 meat patties on top. Serve.

VEAL MARENGO

Yield: 100 servings

Ingredients:

25	pounds veal, cubed
25	medium onions, chopped
1 1/2	pounds butter
6 1/4	cups flour
	salt and pepper to taste
1 1/2	gallons beef stock
1 1/2	cups tomato puree
6	bay leaves, whole
2	gallons sliced mushrooms
1	gallon stuffed green olives, drained (optional)

Toss cubed meat in flour, and cook in butter until lightly browned. Remove meat from pan; add onion, and cook until tender and translucent. Return meat to pan and add remaining ingredients except for mushrooms. Simmer for 1 hour.

Add mushrooms and olives, if desired, and heat for an additional 10 minutes.

VEAL ROMA

Yield: 100 servings

Ingredients:

34	pounds veal shoulder, cubed
2	cups oil
17	cloves garlic, crushed
2 1/2	gallons sliced mushrooms
1	No. 10 can tiny white onions
1	tablespoon salt
1	teaspoon white pepper
68	large tomatoes
2	quarts dry white wine
1	gallon plus 1 cup chicken stock
4	bunches parsley
1	tablespoon thyme
5	bay leaves, whole

Brown veal cubes in oil. Remove meat. Cook garlic, mushrooms, and onions just until soft. Remove vegetables from oil, and mix with meat in casserole; season well. Skin and deseed tomatoes; chop coarsely. Combine oil with wine, stock, and herbs. Simmer until smooth, or strain. Pour over meat and vegetables.

Bake at 325 degrees F for 1 1/2 hours.

VEAL TRÈS ELEGANT

Very Special Occasion Entree

Yield: 100 servings

Ingredients:

100	pieces veal escallops
6	pounds butter
25	medium onions, sliced
8	quarts sliced fresh mushrooms
3	pounds stuffed green olives
3	pounds fresh white bread crumbs
25	eggs
25	oranges, juiced (save rinds for garnish)
1 1/2	cups sherry
3	quarts cream

Melt half of the butter in pan; fry onions until translucent. Add mushrooms, and cook for 2 minutes. Chop half of the olives, and add to pan with bread crumbs and egg. Season to taste.

Place about 1/2 to 1 tablespoon of crumb mixture on each veal escallop, and spread evenly across surface. Roll up meat and secure with a toothpick.

Melt remaining butter in pan, and fry meat rolls until golden and cooked. Put into serving dish and keep hot. Thicken pan juices with flour until a medium paste forms. Add stock slowly, stirring constantly to blend; simmer 1 minute. Add orange juice, sherry, and cream. Bring to very hot temperature; do not boil or it will curdle. Pour over meat.

Garnish with remaining olives, halved, and sprinkle top with strips of orange rind.

SWISS VEAL

Yield: 100 servings

Ingredients:

25 1/2 pounds veal, sliced thin
      seasoned flour (flour with salt, pepper, rosemary, and thyme)
  4 1/4 cups oil
    34 medium onions, sliced
    17 cloves garlic
     3 No. 10 cans tomatoes
     3 tablespoons sugar
 1 1/2 teaspoons rosemary
 1 1/2 teaspoons thyme
     9 pounds Gruyere cheese, sliced
     2 cups grated Parmesan cheese

Toss veal slices in flour and brown in oil. Then remove veal to baking pan; add onions and garlic to original pan, and cook until golden. Puree tomatoes and add to onions with herbs and sugar. Simmer 5 minutes and pour half of this sauce over veal. Top with Gruyere cheese and remaining sauce; sprinkle with Parmesan cheese.

Bake uncovered at 350 degrees F for 45 minutes.

11 POULTRY

THE COOK'S PAINT POT

"You will keep in perfect peace him whose mind is steadfast, because he trusts in you" (Isaiah 26:3).

Busy in my preparations for the Men's Fellowship breakfast, I started toward the refrigerator door. Near it was a pool of shiny grease, which in my haste I did not see. Wham! I slipped, and the bowl of pancake batter I was carrying flew up in the air. Naturally it did not come down nice and neat but dribbled like a basket ball. Pancake batter covered the kitchen floor. The rest of the kitchen crew was in the dining room, and I yelled for assistance, but no one

came. I gingerly stepped around the spilled batter to mix more. I was so angry at myself, I neglected the bacon, and it started to burn. Grease spattered on my arm. "Dear God, help me to be calm," I prayed. Attempting to get a grip on myself, I remembered the following story:

Three artists were asked to paint a picture showing complete peace. One artist painted a picture of a little boy fishing. The boy was lying back against the bank, his toes wiggling, his eyes shut. The water was smooth, not even a ripple could be seen. Another artist painted a picture of a beautiful green meadow, shadowed by large trees. A dozen or more cows placidly nibbled the grass. The third artist painted a picture of a severe storm. The lightning and rain came down in sheets. The wind blew so hard a tree was bent almost to the ground. In the V of one of the branches of this tree was a bird nest with three tiny birds poking their little bills out from under their mother. They were at perfect peace, even though the intense storm raged around them. They were calm and secure, knowing they were completely protected by their mother. That painting was selected as depicting complete peace.

So it is with us when we are under the care of our heavenly Father. The storm may rage around us, and complete chaos may exist (such as that in my kitchen), but when our minds are steadfast on Him, He will keep us in perfect peace. Thank you, Lord.

125

By Dorothy M. Siebert

SESAME DRESSING FOR PORK OR POULTRY

Yield: 100 servings (using #24 scoop)

Ingredients:

- 1 1/2 quarts chicken broth
- 2 quarts chopped celery
- 4 quarts 1/2-inch bread cubes
- 1 quart chopped onions
- 2 cups margarine
- 2 cups sesame seeds, toasted
- 8 tablespoons poultry seasoning
- 16 eggs, beaten slightly
  salt and pepper to taste

Cook onions and celery in margarine. Toss with remaining ingredients. Use a #24 scoop per serving to stuff poultry.

BAKED CHICKEN QUARTERS

Yield: 100 servings

Ingredients:

Seasoning (below)
25 chickens (2 3/4 to 3 pounds each), washed and quartered
6 ounces salt
2 ounces pepper

Salt and pepper underside of chickens; then lay seasoned side down in oven trays. Brush the surface of chickens with melted chicken fat or margarine; sprinkle with seasoning mixture of your choice; and drizzle with about 2 cups of melted margarine or butter. Bake at 350 degrees F for 40 minutes or until done.

SEASONINGS

HAWAIIAN: 3 quarts very fine corn flake crumbs; 2 cups flaked coconut; 4 tablespoons curry powder

ITALIAN: 3 quarts very fine bread crumbs; 4 tablespoons whole Italian herbs or seasoning; salt and pepper to taste

CHEESY GARLIC: 3 quarts very fine bread crumbs; 2 cups grated Parmesan cheese; 2 tablespoons granulated garlic

CHEF'S SPECIAL: 8 ounces salt; 2 ounces each of cracked pepper, paprika, sesame seeds, and poppy seeds; 2 cups Parmesan cheese

CHICKEN PINEAPPLE

Yield: 100 servings

Ingredients:

100 boneless chicken breasts (6 ounces each)
10 ounces soy sauce
6 ounces salt
4 ounces sugar
4 pounds flour
1 No. 10 can crushed pineapple
fat for frying

Combine half of the soy sauce with salt and sugar. Spread over chicken and let stand 1 hour.

Drain chicken; dredge with flour. Brown chicken in hot fat; place in baking pan.

Blend remaining soy sauce with pineapple, and ladle over chicken. Cover; bake in oven at 350 degrees F for 30 minutes or until tender.

CHICKEN PARMESAN

Yield: 100 servings

Ingredients:

	Spaghetti (below)
100	chicken breasts (5 to 6 ounces each)
	Parmesan cheese
	fat for frying
16	cloves garlic, finely chopped
24	ounces flour
7	quarts chicken broth
8	cups dry sherry
4	pounds mushrooms, quartered
4	tablespoons butter
8	lemons, juice only
2	cups water
2	teaspoons salt

Rub chicken pieces with Parmesan cheese. Slowly brown in fat. When golden brown, remove from frying pan and place chicken in baking pan. Pour off fat except for 3 cups. To this reserved fat add the finely chopped garlic cloves; cook until soft but not brown. Blend in the flour until smooth. Add chicken broth and sherry to flour mixture, then mushrooms, butter, lemon juice, water, and salt. Simmer for 10 minutes, stirring constantly until thickened. Adjust salt and pepper to taste.

Pour sauce over chicken in baking pans. Cover and bake at 350 degrees F until tender, about 30 to 40 minutes.

Sprinkle with parsley. Serve with spaghetti and additional Parmesan cheese.

SPAGHETTI

Boil 6 pounds spaghetti in 6 gallons boiling salted water.

DIJON CHICKEN

Yield: 100 servings (2 pieces of meat per serving)

Ingredients:

     200 pieces chicken (breasts, thighs, and legs)
     1/3 cup salt
       4 teaspoons pepper
       4 teaspoons garlic powder
       2 quarts Dijon-style mustard
       2 quarts sour cream
       1 gallon Italian-flavored bread crumbs
       1 quart dried parsley

Sprinkle chicken with salt, pepper, and garlic powder. Combine sour cream with mustard. Spread over chicken, and roll each piece in crumbs. Place in single layer on baking sheets.

Bake at 400 degrees F for 45 minutes, or until done. Dust with parsley before serving.

This is delicious hot or cold for picnics.

ELEGANT GLAZED CHICKEN

Yield: 100 servings

Ingredients:

     100 boned chicken breasts (6 ounces each)
          salt and pepper to taste
       6 tablespoons granulated garlic
       3 tablespoons monosodium glutamate (MSG)
    7 1/2 quarts canned chicken broth
       1 No. 10 can apricot preserves or marmalade
       5 cups white wine

Season chicken breasts with salt and pepper and set in prepared baking pans. Combine garlic, MSG, and broth. Pour over chicken. Cover and bake at 350 degrees F for 45 minutes or until tender.

Combine wine and preserves; spoon over chicken. Bake uncovered at 400 degrees F for 15 minutes, basting often. This should make an attractive glaze when served.

VIRGINIA'S SWEET-SOUR CHICKEN

Yield: 90 servings (1/2 chicken per person)

Ingredients:

Sauce (below)

45 small chickens, split
flour
cloves, cinnamon, rosemary, salt, and pepper
margarine

Dredge chicken in flour; sprinkle slightly with each spice listed. Place on baking tray and drizzle with melted margarine. Bake at 350 degrees F for about 1 hour, or until done. Serve with sauce poured over each portion.

SAUCE

4 cans (46 ounces each) chicken broth
2 3/4 quarts pineapple juice
1 tablespoon ground cloves
1 tablespoon cinnamon
1 tablespoon monosodium glutamate (MSG)
1 1/2 pounds butter
1 quart cider vinegar
6 cups pineapple tidbits
6 cups canned apricots
3 No. 2 cans cranberry jelly

Combine first 7 ingredients and bring to a boil. Thicken with cornstarch until right consistency. (Add more water or more pineapple juice if necessary.) Boil gently 1 minute. Add pineapple, apricots, and cranberry jelly.

ALTERNATE SAUCE

4 cans (26 ounces each) chicken broth
2 3/4 quarts cherry juice
1 1/2 pounds butter
3 quarts *dark* cherries
1 tablespoon cinnamon
1 tablespoon cloves

Combine, cook, and thicken as above.

INDIAN CURRIED CHICKEN

Virginia's Own

Yield: 104 servings

Ingredients:

   Glaze (below)
6 1/2 cups cornstarch
 1 cup curry powder
6 1/2 cups margarine, melted
 1 No. 10 can pie apples, chopped
1 1/2 tablespoons garlic granules
 1/4 cup lemon juice
104 chicken breasts (6 ounces each)

Mix cornstarch and curry powder together; set aside.

Combine pie apples with garlic and lemon juice; set aside.

Open each breast and place 1 tablespoon of apple mixture on it. Close up and shape like a pillow. Dip in cornstarch mixture and place on prepared baking sheet. Baste each breast with 1 tablespoon melted margarine.

Bake at 325 degrees F for about 30 minutes, or until half done. Remove from the oven and spread with 1 tablespoon of glaze. Return to oven 30 minutes more, or until done.

Excellent served with rice pilaf (rice cooked in orange juice and chicken broth) and mushrooms.

GLAZE

 1/2 No. 10 can apple jelly
 2 bottles (24 ounces each) Major Grey's mango chutney

Combine ingredients, rinsing chutney bottles with about 2 tablespoons of water in order to get all of the chutney out of bottles.

LEMON CHICKEN

Yield: 96 servings

Ingredients:

- 10 large cloves garlic, finely chopped
- 3 tablespoons salt
- 6 1/2 cups salad oil
- 3 1/2 cups lemon juice
- 1/2 cup grated lemon peel
- 3 cups finely chopped onions
- 3 tablespoons white pepper
- 4 tablespoons whole thyme
  - fat for frying
- 24 chickens (approximately 2 1/2 pounds each), quartered

Combine first 8 ingredients, and store overnight in refrigerator. Fry chicken pieces until golden brown. Drain. Place in 4 baking pans (12x15x5 inches each), skin side up. Pour sauce over chicken, being sure to coat each piece carefully.

Bake at 325 degrees F for 1 1/2 to 1 3/4 hours. Baste every 1/2 hour with sauce. Serve chicken with sauce.

12 FISH AND SEAFOOD

GIVING ALL

"[Elijah] called to her and asked, 'Would you bring me a little water in a jar so I may have a drink?' As she was going to get it, he called, 'And bring me, please, a piece of bread.'

" 'As surely as the Lord your God lives,' she replied, 'I don't have any bread—only a handful of flour in a jar and a little oil in a jug. I am gathering a few sticks to take home and make a meal for myself and my son, that we may eat it—and die.'

"Elijah said to her, 'Don't be afraid. Go home and do as you have said. But first make a small cake of bread for me from what you have and bring it to me, and then make something for yourself and your son. For this is what the Lord, the God of Israel, says: "The jar of flour will not be used up and the jug of oil will not run dry until the day the Lord gives rain on the land." '

"She went away and did as Elijah had told her. So there was food every day for Elijah and for the woman and her family. For the jar of flour was not used up and the jug of oil did not run dry, in keeping with the word of the Lord spoken by Elijah" (1 Kings 17:10-16).

Dear Lord, thank You for the widow who demonstrated her faith in

You by responding to Elijah's request and willingly giving him her last small amount of flour and oil. Help me also to demonstrate my faith in You as I give to others. And as the unfailing flour and oil show Your inexhaustible resources and Your unfailing ministrations to human need, help me to rely on Your resources when mine fail. Amen

FISH

DILLED HALIBUT

Yield: 100 servings

Ingredients:

- 24 pounds halibut fillets (1 inch thick)
- 6 quarts sour cream
- 1 quart chopped dill pickles
- 1 quart chopped green onions
- 2 cups chopped green peppers
- 1 1/2 cups chopped parsley
- 1 1/2 cups lemon juice
- 2 tablespoons Dijon mustard
- 2 tablespoons basil
- 2 tablespoons salt
- 2 teaspoons pepper

Put fillets on baking pans. Combine remaining ingredients and pour over fish.

Bake at 350 degrees F for 30 minutes.

Garnish with dill pickle fans and parsley sprigs.

BAKED COD MT. HERMON STYLE
WITH TARTAR SAUCE

Yield: 100 servings (5 ounces each)

Ingredients:

> 1 gallon Tartar Sauce (below)
>
> 32 1/2 pounds fresh or frozen cod
> 5 tablespoons lemon parsley salt, divided in half
> 1 gallon fine bread crumbs
> 1 1/2 pounds margarine
> paprika

Place fish on prepared baking sheet. Season liberally with half the lemon parsley salt and allow to stand while combining ingredients for coating. Mix bread crumbs with remaining lemon parsley salt and toss with melted margarine.

Pack crumbs on top of fish. Dust with paprika and bake at 325 degrees F for 30 to 40 minutes, or until no longer transparent but *just* white and flaky. Serve with Tartar Sauce.

TARTAR SAUCE

> 3 quarts mayonnaise
> 1 quart dill pickle relish
> 1/2 cup finely diced onions

Mix together and refrigerate for at least 1 hour.

SEAFOOD

MERMAID'S PINEAPPLE BOAT

A Favorite Ladies' Luncheon!

Yield: 100 servings

Ingredients:

20	pounds jumbo shrimp
6	lemons, juice only
5	bay leaves
1	onion
50	pineapples
6 1/2	pounds lump crabmeat
6 1/2	pounds lump lobster
3	pounds Louis Dressing (page 80)
3	pounds cocktail sauce
3	pounds Russian Dressing
2	No. 10 cans black olives, drained
12	cans (7 ounces each) pimiento strips
	leaf lettuce

Cook shrimp 15 minutes, or until done, in boiling water that has been salted
and flavored with lemon juice, bay leaves, and onion. Drain, cool, peel, and
devein shrimp.

Cut whole pineapple in half lengthwise, leaving frond attached but cutting it
in two. Remove pulp and cut into cubes, discarding core if hard.

Line pineapple boat with colorful leaf lettuce. Place 1 ounce crabmeat at one
end of boat, 4 shrimp in the middle, and 1 ounce lobster at the other end.
Cover crabmeat with Louis Dressing, shrimp with cocktail sauce, and lobster
with Russian Dressing.

Garnish with black olives, pimiento, and sprig of parsley or twist of lemon
slice.

SHRIMP BOAT MEDLEY

Yield: 96 servings (1 bun with 2 ounces salad)

Ingredients:

- 1/4 cup chopped or dehydrated onions or thinly sliced green onions
- 5 pounds fresh or canned shrimp, cooked (or 4 quarts)
- 1 quart mayonnaise
- 2 quarts finely cut celery
- 12 hard-cooked eggs, chopped
- 1/4 cup lemon juice
- 1 cup chopped green peppers
- 1/3 cup salt
- 2 tablespoons pepper
- 96 buns, split and toasted
- 96 tomato slices
- 96 dill pickle slices
  lettuce or sprouts
- 1/2 teaspoon dill or paprika

Combine all ingredients through pepper; toss and chill. On the bottom half of bun place a leaf of lettuce and 1 tomato slice. Top with #20 scoop of shrimp salad.

SUPREME COLD SHRIMP REMOULADE SALAD

Yield: 100 servings

Ingredients:

- 6 cups minced celery
- 6 cups chopped onions
- 4 cups parsley
- 6 cups chopped dill pickles
- 1 1/2 quarts Dijon mustard
- 2 cups vinegar
- 2 cups oil
- 25 pounds shrimp, cooked and peeled
- 12 quarts lettuce (half of it finely shredded)

Combine all ingredients except shrimp and lettuce. Mix and chill.

Put 4 ounces of shrimp on 1/2 cup lettuce greens; top with 1/2 cup of sauce; and serve on whole lettuce leaf.

13 VEGETABLES

FORGIVE MY MESS

O God, I've really made a mess!

You know I had the best of intentions, but somehow it didn't work out.

Lord, maybe I lost sight of my priorities; I don't know.

But right now, Jesus, I need a big helping of Your grace.

Show me, Lord, where to start making it right.

Inspire me so as not to waste Your provisions.

Calm my inner self from my anger and frustration.

And if it wouldn't be asking too much, Lord, give me the grace of a sense of humor.

Thank You and . . . Amen.

By Marilee

OL' VIRGINIA'S BAKED BEANS

Yield: 100 servings

Ingredients:

- 5 No. 10 cans baked beans in tomato sauce (no meat)
- 1/2 gallon molasses
- 2 quarts brown sugar
- 3 tablespoons dry mustard
- 1 cup dry onions
- 2 cups vinegar

Combine all ingredients and put into 2 baking pans, each measuring 12x20x2 inches. Place in slow oven (300 degrees F) for 3 hours. Then uncover and bake at 325 degrees F until beans have absorbed most of the moisture. Beans are done when they are not too soupy and not too dry.

VARIATION: Add 500 lil' wienies or lil' smokies, or cubed ham, pork chops, or leftover pork roast. For an exotic taste that's a favorite, add slices of linguisa.

ZEBRA BEANS

Yield: 100 servings (1/2 cup each)

Ingredients:

- 1 1/2 pounds celery, sliced thinly on diagonal
- 2 pounds onions, chopped
- 1 1/2 pounds butter
- 2 No. 10 cans diagonally cut green beans, undrained
- 2 No. 10 cans diagonally cut wax beans, undrained
- 2 cups finely chopped parsley
- 28 ounces diced pimiento
- salt and pepper to taste

Cook celery and onions in butter till onions are translucent. Heat beans until hot and pour off about half the liquid. Add onions and celery. Serve.

GREEN BEANS ITALIAN STYLE

Yield: 100 servings

Ingredients:

    3   pounds bacon, diced
1 1/2   quarts chopped onions
    4   No. 10 cans green beans (or 12 pounds)
    1   tablespoon salt
    1   quart corn flake crumbs
    1   quart grated Parmesan cheese

Fry bacon until crisp. Drain. In skillet with bacon drippings, cook onions until tender. Drain. Cook or heat green beans.

Toss bacon, onions, and corn flake crumbs with beans. Gently fold in cheese. Serve immediately.

BAKED PEAS AND CARROTS DREAM

Yield: 100 servings (1/2 cup each)

Ingredients:

    12   pounds frozen peas or peas and carrots, defrosted, or 4 No. 10 cans
     2   cups butter (first amount)
     2   cups flour
     4   teaspoons salt
     2   teaspoons pepper
     1   tablespoon Worcestershire sauce
          dash tabasco
     2   quarts liquid (from peas or light chicken broth)
     1   can (50 ounces) condensed cream of mushroom soup
     2   quarts grated American cheese
     1   cup butter (second amount)
1 1/2   cups soft bread crumbs

Make cream sauce with first amount of butter, flour, seasonings, and liquid; add mushroom soup. Cook until thickened, stirring constantly. Add cheese. Gently fold in peas (or peas and carrots). Pour into greased baking pans.

Combine last cup of butter with bread crumbs and sprinkle over peas. Bake at 350 degrees F for 45 minutes, or until bubbly.

SUFFERIN' SUCCOTASH VEGGIE BAKE

Yield: 100 servings (1/2 cup each)

Ingredients:

> 2 No. 10 cans cream style corn
> 2 quarts frozen or canned lima beans
> 2 cups chopped onions
> 2 cups chopped green pepper
> 1/2 cup freshly diced parsley
> 2 quarts seasoned bread crumbs
> 2 cups butter, melted
> 1 cup water (approximately)

Mix first 5 ingredients and place in 2 baking pans, each measuring 12x20 inches.

Combine bread crumbs with butter and add water. Sprinkle over corn and bean mix. Cover with foil.

Bake at 350 degrees F for 45 minutes. Uncover and bake another 15 minutes until lightly browned.

EMERALDS-IN-SNOW CREAMED PEAS

Yield: 100 servings (1/2 cup each)

Ingredients:

> 2 pounds bacon, fried crisp and crumbled (save fat drippings)
> 1 quart finely chopped onions, cooked in butter or bacon fat until translucent; drained
> 3 cups flour
> 6 quarts milk
> 4 No. 10 cans green peas (or 12 pounds frozen peas, cooked)
> salt and white pepper to taste
> 1 tablespoon dill weed
> 1/2 teaspoon tabasco

To bacon drippings add flour; stir until smooth. Add milk, stirring constantly over heat. Cook until thickened.

Gently fold in peas and seasonings to taste. Barely heat through.

LEAPING BEANS

Yield: 100 servings (1/2 cup each)

Ingredients:

> Cream Sauce (below)
> 4 No. 10 cans cut green beans, drained of half their juice
> 1 cup chopped onions
> paprika, parsley, or freshly chopped chives for garnish

Lightly cook onions until translucent. Heat beans in their juice. When hot, drain and combine with onions.

Serve beans with a spoonful of cream sauce, sprinkled with onions, and dusted with paprika, parsley, or freshly chopped chives.

CREAM SAUCE

> 1 1/2 cups melted butter
> 1 1/2 cups flour
> 1 gallon plus 2 cups milk
> 3 cups mustard (Use Dijon or mustard with seeds for extra zest.)
> 2 teaspoons salt
> 4 tablespoons cream style horseradish

Combine butter and flour, and cook over low heat for 5 minutes. Gradually add milk. Cook until thickened or till sauce bubbles slightly. Add mustard, salt, and horseradish. Keep warm.

POTATOES AU GRATIN

Yield: 120 servings (1/4 cup each)

Ingredients:

> 2 quarts corn flake crumbs
> 2 cups margarine, melted
> 4 gallons instant potatoes, sliced, cooked, and drained, or 20 pounds cooked fresh potatoes
> 1 1/2 gallons white sauce
> 1/2 cup green onions, sliced
> 4 cans (50 ounces each) condensed cheddar cheese soup
> 1/4 cup ham soup base

Mix crumbs with margarine and set aside.

Grease 4 pans (20x12x2 1/2 inches each) and layer about 5 pounds of cooked potatoes in each one.

To hot white sauce, add cheddar cheese soup, ham soup base, and green onions. Pour about 3 quarts of sauce over each pan of potatoes. Sprinkle each pan with 2 cups corn flake crumbs.

Bake at 400 degrees F for 25 minutes.

POTATO PANCAKES
WITH GERMAN PINK APPLESAUCE

Yield: 100 servings (3 pancakes, 3 inches each, per serving)

Ingredients:

>   German Pink Applesauce (below)

- 5 cups eggs
- 6 quarts milk
- 4 tablespoons salt
- 1 teaspoon pepper
- 7 cups instant mashed potatoes
- 1 cup flour
- 4 teaspoons baking powder
- 1 cup finely chopped onions
- 4 tablespoons finely chopped parsley
- 1/8 teaspoon nutmeg

Beat eggs slightly; add milk and seasonings. Combine dry ingredients and add gradually to milk mixture. Add the remaining ingredients.

Oil griddle. When griddle is hot, fry pancakes, using about 1 tablespoon of oil per pancake. Brown on both sides, turning only once.

Serve with German Pink Applesauce.

GERMAN PINK APPLESAUCE

- 2 No. 10 cans applesauce (or 6 quarts fresh)
- 1 cup strawberry flavored gelatin (or 6 ounces red hot cinnamon candy) melted into applesauce

Combine ingredients and serve warm.

POTATOES O'BRIEN

Yield: 100 servings

Ingredients:

- 10 pounds frozen hash browned potatoes, thawed
- 10 cups grated American cheese
- 3 cups chopped green peppers
- 3 cups chopped onions
- 2 1/2 cups chopped pimiento
- 1 cup flour
- 6 tablespoons salt
- 1 teaspoon white pepper
- 1 quart plus 1 1/2 cups half-and-half
- 1 cup diced parsley

Combine all ingredients except half-and-half and parsley. Put into 3 pans (12x20 inches each). Pour cream over the potatoes. Cover with foil and bake at 400 degrees F for 30 minutes. Remove foil and continue baking another 50 to 60 minutes, or until well browned. Dust with parsley.

SPINACH SOUFFLÉ

Yield: 108 servings

Ingredients:

- 24 pounds frozen chopped spinach
- 3/4 cup butter
- 3/4 cup flour
-    salt and pepper to taste
- 1/2 teaspoon nutmeg
- 6 cups hot chicken stock, or milk
- 3 cups Parmesan cheese
- 3/4 cup butter
- 36 egg yolks, well beaten
- 48 egg whites, beaten stiff

Melt butter in saucepan; add spinach. Cover and cook until all water has boiled away.

Combine flour, salt, pepper, and nutmeg; add 1 cup hot stock, stir until smooth. Add the remaining hot stock and bring to a gentle boil, stirring constantly until thickened, about 15 to 20 minutes.

Fold in spinach gently, and continue heating until hot. Remove from heat.

Add 1 cup Parmesan cheese and beaten egg yolks. Blend thoroughly. Cool.

Fold in stiffly beaten egg whites. Pour into 2 hotel pans; set in hot water bath. Smooth surface into shape of dome. Sprinkle rest of cheese over top, and drizzle with remaining melted butter.

Bake at 325 to 350 degrees F for 40 to 50 minutes.

INDIAN SQUASH MEDLEY

Yield: 100 servings (1/2 cup each)

Ingredients:

- 3 quarts sliced onions
- 3 1/2 pounds butter
- 18 pounds squash (any combination of zucchini, summer, butternut, or banana)
- 1 No. 10 can tomatoes
- 3 pounds grated cheese
- 6 tablespoons salt
- 1 teaspoon pepper
- 1 tablespoon summer savory
- 2 quarts bread crumbs

Cook onions in half of butter. Add squash and gently stir-fry until well blended and glazed with butter. Use more butter if necessary. Add remaining ingredients except for bread crumbs. Put squash mixture in as many pans as necessary to make shallow depth (dividing mixture among 4 greased steam table pans should work).

Melt remaining butter in large skillet. Add bread crumbs; stir until golden brown. Sprinkle evenly over each pan of vegetables.

Bake at 350 degrees F for 30 minutes.

POTATOES ROMANOFF

Yield: 100 servings (1/2 cup each)

Ingredients:

10	pounds green onions, sliced
6	cups butter
120	eggs (or 1 gallon plus 2 quarts)
16	cups grated sharp cheddar cheese (or 4 pounds)
3 1/4	cups milk
3	cups sour cream
3	cups chopped fresh parsley
1	tablespoon salt
1	teaspoon pepper
12	pounds potatoes, cooked with skins on; grated paprika

Cook onions in butter until soft. Beat eggs slightly and combine with half the cheese, milk, sour cream, and seasonings. Gently fold into grated potatoes. Press potatoes gently into baking pans; top with remaining cheese and dust with paprika.

Bake in 350 degrees F oven for 50 minutes or until set.

BAKED SPINACH SQUARES

Yield: 100 servings

Ingredients:

21	pounds frozen chopped spinach, thawed and well drained
6 1/2	cups eggs
5 1/3	cups fine crumbs
1/2	cup vinegar
1	tablespoon granulated onion
2	teaspoons salt
1/4	teaspoon white pepper
1 1/2	quarts Parmesan cheese
1	quart shredded cheddar cheese

Mix all ingredients together except for cheddar cheese and half the crumbs. Place in 2 pans (13x22 inches each). Combine remaining half of crumbs with cheddar cheese and place on top of spinach mixture.

Bake at 300 degrees F for 40 minutes or until the crumbs are light brown.

14 DESSERTS

*TABLE PRAYERS
FOR RETURNING THANKS
AFTER MEALS*

Let us give thanks to the Lord
    for He is good,
For His mercy endures forever. Amen

To God, who gives us daily bread,
A thankful song we'll raise,
And pray that He who sends our food
Will fill our hearts with praise. Amen*

For all these gifts, O Lord,
Make us truly thankful. Amen*

Bless the Lord, O my soul, and all that
    is within me,
Bless His holy name.
Bless the Lord, O my soul,
And forget not all His benefits. Amen

Thank You for this meal, dear Lord,
Thank You for Your living Word.
As I pray with head bowed low,
In Your service let me grow.†

As these gifts the body nourish,
May our souls in graces flourish
Till with saints in heavenly splendor
At Your feast our thanks we render.‡

*From *Dear Father in Heaven,* copyright © 1963
by Concordia Publishing House, p. 13.

†From *Prayers for the Very Young Child,* copyright © 1981
by Concordia Publishing House, p. 50.

‡Adapted from "Feed Your Children, God Most Holy,"
Lutheran Worship, copyright © 1982 by Concordia
Publishing House.

O Jesus, Bread of Life from heaven,
Bless this food You here have given!

For all Your gifts, dear God, so free,
To You we ever thankful be. Amen*

*From *Dear Father in Heaven*, copyright © 1963
by Concordia Publishing House, p. 13.

CAKES

APPLESAUCE CAKE

Yield: 100 servings (2 pans, 18x26 inches each)

Ingredients:

- 4 quarts flour
- 7 3/4 cups sugar
- 2 tablespoons baking soda
- 1/4 cup baking powder
- 2 tablespoons cinnamon
- 1 1/2 tablespoons cloves
- 2 tablespoons salt
- 3 1/2 cups shortening
- 5 cups raisins
- 9 cups canned applesauce
- 1 1/2 tablespoons vanilla
- 10 eggs

Sift dry ingredients together. Add shortening; mix until texture is like corn-meal. Add raisins and half of applesauce. Add vanilla and remaining apple-sauce. Mix well. Add eggs, stirring just to blend.

Grease and flour 2 pans and divide batter between them.

Bake at 350 degrees F for about 35 minutes or until cakes test done.

PINEAPPLE UPSIDE DOWN CAKE

Yield: 100 servings, (2 pans, 18x26 inches each)

Ingredients:

- 1 1/2 quarts brown sugar
- 3 cups butter
- 1 No. 10 can pineapple (crushed, sliced, or diced)
  nut meats or Maraschino cherries (optional)
- 2 cups shortening
- 1 1/2 quarts granulated sugar
- 13 eggs
- 3 1/2 tablespoons vanilla
- 3 1/3 quarts flour
- 6 2/3 teaspoons baking powder
- 6 3/4 cups milk
- 3/4 teaspoon salt

Divide butter between pans and spread thickly on bottom. Divide brown sugar between pans and spread evenly over bottoms. Thoroughly drain pineapple and spread over sugar. If desired, arrange nut meats or Maraschino cherries throughout pineapple. Set prepared pans aside.

Cream shortening and sugar. Add eggs and vanilla. Sift dry ingredients together and add gradually to rest of batter alternately with milk. Pour batter into prepared pans using about 5-1/2 pounds per pan.

Bake at 350 degrees F for 30 to 35 minutes or until golden brown and toothpick comes out clean when inserted into center of cake.

Invert hot pans onto serving sheets. Scrape out over the cakes any melted topping from pans. Cool and serve with whipped cream.

LAZY DAISY OATMEAL CAKE

Yield: 100 servings (2 cobbler pans, cut 5x10)

Ingredients:

Lazy Daisy Frosting (below)

2	quarts boiling water
6 2/3	cups oats or wheat flakes
3 1/3	cups soft margarine
6 2/3	cups granulated sugar
6 2/3	cups packed brown sugar
2	tablespoons vanilla
13	eggs
2 1/2	quarts flour
2	tablespoons plus 2/3 teaspoon baking soda
1	tablespoon salt
1	tablespoon plus 2 teaspoons cinnamon
1 1/2	teaspoons nutmeg

Pour boiling water over oats; stir and allow to stand for 20 minutes. Cream together margarine, sugar, vanilla, and eggs. Add oat mixture and blend well.

Mix flour, soda, salt, and spices. Blend with rest of mixture. Pour batter into the 2 prepared pans. Bake at 350 degrees F for 50 to 55 minutes. Frost with Lazy Daisy Frosting.

COCOA OATMEAL CAKE: Increase boiling water to 8 3/4 cups. Use 1 1/4 cups cocoa in place of cinnamon and nutmeg.

LAZY DAISY FROSTING

Yield: enough for 2 pans

1 1/2	cups butter
3 1/3	cups packed brown sugar
1 1/4	cups half-and-half or canned milk
3 1/3	cups chopped nuts
5	cups flaked coconut

Combine all ingredients. Cook until sugar dissolves; spread on cake. *Or* spread uncooked on cake; broil until bubbly. Serve warm or cold.

INKY CHOCOLATE CAKE

Yield: 100 servings (2 pans, 18x26 inches each)

Ingredients:

>   4 1/2 cups cocoa
>   2 quarts hot water
>   2 1/4 cups shortening
>   2 1/2 quarts sugar
>   23 eggs
>   3 tablespoons vanilla
>   3 quarts flour
>   2 tablespoons baking powder
>   2 1/2 tablespoons baking soda
>   2 tablespoons salt

Dissolve cocoa in hot water. Cream shortening and sugar. Add eggs and vanilla. Sift dry ingredients together; add to creamed batter alternately with cocoa-water mixture.

Divide batter between 2 pans. Bake at 350 degrees F for 30 minutes or until tests done.

PUMPKIN SPICE CAKE

Yield: 80 pieces (1 sheet cake, 18x26 inches, cut 10x8)

Ingredients:

>   3 cups seedless raisins
>   2 cups chopped walnuts
>   4 cups sifted flour
>   4 teaspoons baking soda
>   1 teaspoon salt
>   4 teaspoons ground cloves
>   4 teaspoons cinnamon
>   2 teaspoons ginger
>   8 eggs, beaten till light and lemon colored
>   4 cups sugar
>   2 cups salad oil
>   2 pounds pumpkin

Toss first 8 ingredients together and set aside.

Gradually add sugar to eggs until thick and light. At low speed, blend in oil and pumpkin.

Stir flour mixture into wet mixture until well blended.

Bake 50 minutes in prepared pan at 325 to 350 degrees F.

Ice with cream cheese frosting.

SUNSHINE CAKE

Yield: 80 servings (1 sheet cake, 17x26 inches, cut 8x10)

Ingredients:

- 3 egg whites
- 3/4 teaspoon cream of tartar
- 6 tablespoons sugar
- 4 cups flour
- 2 1/2 cups sugar
- 1 1/2 teaspoons cinnamon
- 1 teaspoon salt
- 1 1/2 teaspoons baking soda
- 3/4 teaspoon baking powder
- 1 1/2 cups salad oil
- 3 egg yolks
- 3 3/4 cups grated carrots
- 1 1/2 teaspoons vanilla

Beat egg whites with cream of tartar until stiff peaks are formed. Set aside.

Sift flour once; measure and sift again with remaining dry ingredients.

In mixer beat egg yolks; then add oil; beat for 1 minute. Add dry ingredients and beat 2 minutes. Add carrots and vanilla; beat for 2 more minutes.

Fold in egg white mixture. Pour into prepared pan and bake at 350 degrees F for 40 to 45 minutes.

Frost with Sunshine Frosting (page 158).

CHOCOLATE PARADISE CAKE

Yield: 96 servings (12 layer cake pans, 9 inches each, or 2 oblong layer cake pans, 17x26 inches each)

Ingredients:

- 2 1/2 cups unsweetened chocolate
- 2 1/2 quarts cake flour, sifted (or 10 cups)
- 2 1/4 quarts sugar (or 9 cups)
- 2 1/2 tablespoons baking soda
- 2 tablespoons salt
- 3 cups oil
- 1 quart milk
- 1 1/2 tablespoons vanilla
- 3 cups milk
- 15 eggs

Melt chocolate; cool. Sift dry ingredients together; combine in mixer at low speed. Add oil, half of milk, and vanilla. Mix until well blended and smooth. Add rest of milk, eggs, and chocolate; beat until blended.

Divide batter between 2 pans measuring 17x26 inches or allow 17 ounces for each 9-inch cake pan.

Bake at 350 degrees F for 30 minutes or until cakes test done.

POPPY SEED CAKE

Yield: 128 servings (16 layer cake pans, 9 inches each)

Ingredients:

Filling (below)

- 1 1/2 quarts milk
- 1 1/2 quarts poppy seeds
- 1 1/4 quarts butter or margarine
- 3 quarts sugar
- 4 1/2 quarts cake flour, sifted
- 1 1/2 tablespoons baking powder
- 32 egg whites

Pour milk over seeds and let stand for 2 hours. Cream butter and sugar till fluffy. Sift dry ingredients together. Add dry ingredients alternately with wet ingredients to butter and sugar. Set aside.

Beat egg whites until stiff but not dry. Fold into batter.

Portion about 1 pound, 3 ounces of batter into each cake pan. Bake at 350 degrees F for about 25 to 30 minutes. Cool thoroughly. Slice each layer in half. Spread bottom half of layer with filling and place top half on it. Cut each filled layer into 8 wedge-shaped pieces and sprinkle with powdered sugar. Serve same day as made or refrigerate.

FILLING

32	egg yolks
1 1/4	quarts sugar
1	cup cornstarch
2	teaspoons salt
3	quarts milk, scalded
1	cup chopped pecans
3	tablespoons vanilla

Beat yolks until pale in color; add sugar, cornstarch, and salt. Gradually add scalded milk. Slowly bring to boil, stirring constantly. Cook until thickened. Remove from heat and cool. When cool, add vanilla and nuts. Chill before using.

BANANA CAKE

Yield: 100 servings (2 pans, 18x26 inches each)

Ingredients:

2 2/3	cups margarine
2	quarts sugar
2	tablespoons vanilla
13	eggs
1 1/4	quarts mashed bananas (about 2 1/2 pounds)
3 1/2	quarts flour
6	tablespoons baking powder
2	teaspoons baking soda
2	tablespoons salt
1 1/2	quarts buttermilk
3	cups chopped nuts

Blend shortening, sugar, and vanilla. Add eggs and beat until smooth. Sift dry ingredients together. Set aside. To sugar batter add banana pulp. Then add flour mixture alternately with buttermilk.

Bake at 350 degrees F for 30 to 35 minutes or until cakes test done.

DANISH CRUMB CAKE

Yield: 140 servings (2 pans, 18x26 inches each, cut 7x10)

Ingredients:

       13 cups flour
    13 1/2 cups rolled oats
       11 cups brown sugar
        2 1/4 pounds butter
        2 1/2 teaspoons salt
        2 tablespoons plus 1 teaspoon baking soda
        7 cups brown sugar
        5 cups water
        1 No. 10 can fruit
        6 1/2 ounces cornstarch

Mix first 6 ingredients together until crumbly. Divide into 2 parts. Sprinkle bottom of sprayed pans with the first half of crumb mixture, reserving second portion for topping.

Combine brown sugar, water, fruit, and cornstarch in sauce pan and bring to boil, stirring until thick.

Pour this fruit mixture over crumbs in pan. Top with second portion of dry crumb mixture.

Bake at 400 degrees F for 20 to 25 minutes.

FROSTINGS AND FILLINGS

VIRGINIA'S VERY BEST CHOCOLATE GLAZE

Yield: 144 servings

Ingredients:

- 12 ounces unsweetened chocolate
- 6 ounces butter
- 6 cups sugar
- 3 cups canned milk
- 12 ounces unsweetened chocolate
- 4 tablespoons vanilla

Melt chocolate and butter in double boiler over low heat.

Remove from heat and add sugar slowly; gradually add canned milk. Beat until smooth.

Return to low heat and bring to a boil. Remove from heat and add remaining chocolate. Stir until melted; add vanilla. Cool before using.

CHOCOLATE PEANUT BUTTER FROSTING

Yield: 5 pounds (about 50 servings; frosts 4 two-layer cakes, 8 inches each)

Ingredients:

- 8 ounces semisweet chocolate
- 1/2 cup butter
- 1 gallon powdered sugar
- 1/2 teaspoon salt
- 1 1/2 cups milk
- 1 tablespoon vanilla
- 1 1/4 cups peanut butter

Melt chocolate in double boiler over hot water. Mix in peanut butter and set aside. Cream sugar with salt, milk, and vanilla until smooth. Add chocolate mixture.

NOTE: Frosting stores well in refrigerator. Before using it, however, bring frosting to room temperature and beat well to make it spreadable.

CHOCOLATE FROSTING

Yield: frosts 6 two-layer cakes, 9 inches each, or 3 sheet cakes, 26x17 inches
each

Ingredients:

>   5 quarts powdered sugar
>   3 3/4 cups cocoa
>   1 1/2 cups butter
>   1/2 teaspoon salt
>   2 tablespoons vanilla
>   3 cups milk

Cream butter with sugar; add vanilla. Gradually add cocoa and salt. Add milk
slowly (heated milk will gloss the frosting more). Add a few teaspoons more
milk, if necessary, to make good consistency.

NOTE: Frosting stores well in refrigerator. Before using it, however, bring
frosting to room temperature and beat well to make it spreadable.

SUNSHINE FROSTING

Yield: frosts 1 cake, 17x26 inches

Ingredients:

>   2 cups smooth cottage cheese*
>   5 1/4 cups powdered sugar
>   3/4 cup butter
>   2 1/4 cups coconut
>   3/4 cup chopped pecans or walnuts
>   3/4 cup raisins (optional)
>   2 1/4 teaspoons vanilla

Cream first 5 ingredients together in order listed. Beat at high speed until
light and fluffy. Add nuts and raisins, if desired.

* *If smooth cottage cheese is not available in your area, whirl regular cottage cheese in a
blender until smooth.*

CHOCOLATE FILLING FOR CAKE

Yield: 2 quarts (enough for 2 layer cakes, 9 inches each)

Ingredients:

      1   quart water
      3   cups nonfat dry milk
3 to 4   squares unsweetened chocolate
      1   cup granulated sugar
      1   cup flour
   1/2   teaspoon salt
      4   eggs, well beaten
   1/2   cup butter
      2   cups powdered sugar
2 1/2   teaspoons vanilla

Put water, dry milk, and grated unsweetened chocolate in double boiler, mixing to blend. Heat until chocolate melts and blends.

Combine sugar, flour, and salt; add to hot milk mixture. Bring to boil slowly. Add a small amount of hot mixture to beaten yolks, gradually adding more until mixture is hot and smooth. Stir into remaining filling. Return to heat and gently boil for 2 more minutes. Remove from heat.

Cream butter with powdered sugar and vanilla; beat heavily until fluffy. Whip into chocolate pudding a little at a time.

COOKIES

BROWNIES

160

Yield: 144 large brownies

Ingredients:

19	eggs
4	pounds plus 8 ounces sugar
2 1/4	pounds butter or margarine, melted
1 1/2	pounds cake flour
15	ounces cocoa
2	teaspoons salt
2 1/2	tablespoons vanilla
1	pound walnuts, chopped

Beat eggs at high speed until light (about 5 minutes). Add sugar at low speed until it is mixed with eggs, then beat on high speed for 5 minutes.

Add melted butter and beat at high speed for 5 more minutes.

Gently stir in dry ingredients; beat with paddle for 2 minutes.

Add nuts and vanilla to blend. Bake at 325 degrees F for 25 to 35 minutes in 2 large shallow pans, measuring 18x26 inches each.

RASPBERRY ALMOND COOKIES

Yield: 250 cookies using #70 scoop; 375 cookies using #100 scoop

Ingredients:

2 1/2	cups butter
1 2/3	cups sugar
1 1/4	teaspoons salt
2 1/2	teaspoons vanilla
5	egg yolks
5	cups flour
4	cups chopped almonds
	raspberry jam

Cream together softened butter with sugar, salt, and vanilla. Add egg yolks and flour.

Chill until firm. Form cookies into small balls (using #100 or #70 scoop). Roll in finely chopped almonds.

Depress center with fingertip and fill with raspberry jam.

Bake at 300 degrees F for 10 to 12 minutes. Cookies should remain a light color.

CHOCOLATE CRINKLE COOKIES

Yield: 300 cookies (using #30 scoop)

Ingredients:

- 2 1/2 pounds shortening
- 8 pounds plus 5 ounces sugar
- 3 tablespoons vanilla
- 1 1/4 pounds chocolate (paste)
- 1 pound plus 14 ounces eggs
- 5 pounds flour
- 6 tablespoons plus 2 teaspoons baking powder
- 1 1/2 tablespoons salt
- 3 1/3 cups milk
- 5 cups walnuts, chopped

Mix shortening with sugar and vanilla; beat until fluffy. Add chocolate, then eggs (one at a time).

Sift dry ingredients together. Add to above mixture alternately with milk.

Chill dough at least 3 hours (preferably overnight).

Scoop out balls of dough with #30 scoop. Roll in powdered sugar. Place on baking sheet.

Bake at 350 degrees F for 15 minutes.

NOTE: These cookies are a soft dough and must be well chilled. They will crackle on top and must be rolled in sugar for prettiest effect.

CHOCOLATE CHIP COOKIES

Yield: 190 cookies (using #24 scoop)

Ingredients:

    5 cups brown sugar
    5 cups granulated sugar
    3 cups shortening
    3 cups margarine
   10 eggs
   10 cups flour
   15 cups fine bread crumbs
    2 tablespoons baking soda
    2 tablespoons salt
    2 pounds chocolate chips
    2 cups chopped nuts
 3 1/2 tablespoons vanilla

Mix sugars, shortening, and margarine together until creamy. Beat in eggs. In a separate bowl combine flour, bread crumbs, baking soda, and salt. Add to sugar mixture and beat until blended. Stir in chocolate chips, nuts, and vanilla.

Bake at 375 degrees F for 10 to 12 minutes.

TOLL HOUSE COOKIES

Yield: 100 cookies (using #40 scoop)

Ingredients:

 3 1/2 cups butter
    3 cups brown sugar
    3 cups granulated sugar
    8 eggs
  1/4 cup vanilla
 2 3/4 quarts flour (or 2 3/4 pounds)
    2 tablespoons salt
 1 1/4 tablespoons baking powder
    4 cups chopped nuts
 1 1/4 quarts semisweet chocolate chips

Blend butter with sugars. Add eggs and vanilla; blend. Sift together dry ingredients and add to sugar mixture. Add nuts and chips.

Drop onto baking sheet, using #40 scoop. Bake at 350 degrees F for 8 to 12 minutes.

VIRGINIA'S BEST OATMEAL COOKIES

Yield: 180 cookies (using #24 scoop)

Ingredients:

- 3 pounds margarine
- 3 pounds plus 2 ounces brown sugar
- 4 pounds granulated sugar
- 2 tablespoons vanilla
- 12 eggs
- 2 1/4 pounds flour, sifted
- 2 tablespoons salt
- 2 tablespoons baking powder
- 2 gallons plus 2 cups quick oats

Cream margarine and sugars until light and fluffy. Add vanilla and eggs; mix well.

Combine dry ingredients thoroughly before adding to batter. Add oats; mix until combined. Do not overmix.

To make 180 (large) cookies, use #24 scoop to portion dough; to make medium-sized cookies, use #40 scoop. Bake at 375 degrees F for 12 to 15 minutes or until evenly light brown.

If desired, cookies can be baked in a pan. Divide 10-1/2 pounds of mixture among pregreased pans measuring 25x17 inches each. Spread evenly and thump pan several times to settle. Bake at 350 degrees F for 25 to 30 minutes. Midway through baking period, turn pan so cookies will brown evenly. Cut 8x10 to make 80 pieces per pan.

VARIATION: Add 4 1/2 cups butterscotch chips, chopped coconut, raisins, nuts, or any combination of these to batter.

WHITE OATMEAL COOKIES

Yield: 5 dozen

Ingredients:

1 cup sugar
1 cup margarine or butter
1/2 cup sour milk
2 eggs
1 cup raisins
1 teaspoon baking soda
1 teaspoon salt
2 cups oatmeal
2 cups flour

Mix well. Bake at 350 degrees F until light brown.

OATMEAL COOKIES II

Yield: 10 dozen

Ingredients:

2 cups margarine
2 cups granulated sugar
2 cups brown sugar
4 eggs
3 cups flour
2 teaspoons baking soda
2 teaspoons salt
6 cups oats
2 teaspoons vanilla

Cream together softened margarine with sugars. Add eggs, one at a time; stir in flour and remaining ingredients.

Refrigerate overnight in log-shapped rolls. Cut into slices. Bake at 375 degrees F for 10 minutes.

VIRGINIA'S VERY BEST
NO-ROLL SUGAR COOKIES

Yield: 300 or 600 cookies (using #24 scoop)

Ingredients (300 cookies):

   3 quarts powdered sugar
   3 cups granulated sugar
   6 pounds margarine
 12 eggs
6 1/4 quarts flour*
   4 tablespoons baking soda
   4 tablespoons cream of tartar
   1 tablespoon salt
1 1/2 tablespoons vanilla
1 1/2 teaspoons almond extract

Ingredients (600 cookies):

   6 quarts powdered sugar
   6 cups granulated sugar
 12 pounds margarine
 24 eggs
12 1/2 quarts flour*
   8 tablespoons baking soda
   8 tablespoons cream of tartar
   2 tablespoons salt
   3 tablespoons vanilla
   1 tablespoon almond extract

Cream sugars with margarine until light and fluffy. Add eggs, one at a time, and mix well. Sift together dry ingredients, then combine with sugar mixture. Add flavorings.

Using #24 scoop, drop dough onto pans; dust lightly with granulated sugar. Bake at 375 degrees F for 20 minutes.

Whole wheat flour can be substituted. Cookies will be tan colored but nutritionally good.

PIES

CHERRY PIE

Yield: 20 pies, 10 inches each

Ingredients:

- 30 pounds frozen, pitted, sour red cherries
- 3 ounces red food coloring
- 3 pounds corn syrup
- 11 ounces cornstarch
- 1 quart water
- 5 pounds sugar

Thaw cherries until there is 2 1/2 quarts of juice collected. Mix juice with corn syrup and red food coloring; bring to boil. Add cornstarch to cold water gradually; pour into boiling juices rapidly, stirring quickly with whip until smooth and clear. Add sugar and bring *just* to boil. Pour over cherries, gently folding them in.

Use 24 ounces of filling for each unbaked pie shell. Cover with top crust. Cut slits in crust to allow steam to escape.

Dust lightly with granulated sugar.

Bake in 400 degrees F oven for 45 minutes.

STRAWBERRY ICE CREAM PIE

Yield: 96 servings (12 pies, 10 inches each, 8 slices per pie)

Ingredients:

- 6 quarts corn flake crumbs
- 2 cups sugar
- 4 teaspoons cinnamon
- 2 pounds butter
- 4 gallons vanilla ice cream
- 6 quarts strawberry preserves
- 12 lemons, grated rind only
- 3 quarts chopped apples

Mix crumbs, sugar, cinnamon, and butter. Press into 12 buttered pie pans. Chill.

Soften ice cream. Layer 2 1/2 cups ice cream into each pie shell. Freeze.

Combine preserves, lemon rind, and apples. Divide into 2 containers. Then divide the contents of 1 of the 2 containers evenly amongst the 12 pies, spreading the mixture over the surface of the ice cream. Next, layer an additional 2 1/4 cups of ice cream over this fruit mixture. Spread the remaining container of fruit over the pies. Freeze until hard.

BASIC VANILLA CREAM PIE FILLING

Yield: 12 pies (3 1/2 cups per pie)

Ingredients:

- 1 gallon plus 2 quarts hot milk
- 4 pounds plus 14 ounces sugar
- 1 pound plus 2 ounces cornstarch
- 3 quarts cold milk
- 1 ounce salt
- 3 3/4 cups egg yolks
- 15 ounces butter
- 2 tablespoons plus 3/4 teaspoon vanilla

Add sugar to hot milk; heat until scalding. Mix cornstarch with cold milk. Add to hot milk mixture, stirring rapidly until smooth and thickened. Cook 15 minutes, stirring often.

Mix egg yolks with salt. Add some hot mixture to eggs, whipping to keep smooth. Slowly return to remaining hot mixture, stirring constantly. Bring back to barely a simmer. Turn off heat. Cool; add vanilla. Stir often until pudding is room temperature. Refrigerate.

COCONUT CREAM PIE: Add 1 pound flaked coconut when vanilla is added.

BANANA CREAM PIE: Slice 12 large bananas diagonally; fold bananas into filling when it is thoroughly cool.

PINEAPPLE CREAM: Add 3 quarts well-drained crushed pineapple.

CHOCOLATE CREAM: Increase sugar by 2 1/2 pounds. Mix with 14 ounces cocoa. Proceed as directed.

LUSCIOUS LEMON ANGEL PIE

Yield: 30 servings (5 pies, 9 inches each) or 48 servings (1 rectangular pan, cut 8x6)

Ingredients:

           Topping (below)
           Filling (below)

  20 egg whites (or 2 1/4 cups)
1 1/4 quarts sugar
1 1/4 teaspoons cream of tartar
   2 teaspoons vanilla
 1/4 teaspoon almond extract

To make meringue crust, beat egg whites until foamy. Mix sugar with cream of tartar thoroughly and gradually add to egg whites. Add vanilla and almond extract. Continue beating egg whites until stiff peaks can be made and sugar is thoroughly dissolved. Spread meringue in buttered pie plates, mounding it higher toward the edges. Bake at 225 degrees F for 1 hour. Allow to stand in oven with door ajar until completely cooled.

Spread whipped topping over bottom of meringue, reserving enough for topping over filling. Refrigerate pies overnight.

Pour lemon filling over whipped cream in meringue shell. Cover with thin coat of more whipped cream topping. Sprinkle with grated lemon rind.

TOPPING

1 1/4 cups whipping cream
 1/2 cup sugar
  1 teaspoon vanilla

Beat whipping cream until stiff. Gradually add sugar, then vanilla.

FILLING

  20 egg yolks (or 1 2/3 cups)
1 1/4 cups sugar
1 1/4 cups lemon juice

Beat yolks until light. Add sugar and lemon juice. Bring to boil in double boiler over water until thick. Chill.

PECAN PIE

Yield: 108 servings (18 pies, 8 inches each)

Ingredients:

    54 eggs (or 9 cups)
2 1/4 cups butter, melted
2 1/4 cups flour
    2 tablespoons vanilla
2 1/4 teaspoons salt
    2 quarts plus 1 cup sugar
    7 quarts plus 3 cups dark corn syrup
    7 quarts plus 3 cups pecans
  18 pie shells, unbaked

Beat eggs with mixer; add melted butter, flour, vanilla, salt, sugar, and syrup.

Sprinkle about 1 1/2 cups nuts over bottom of each pastry shell. Divide syrup mixture among the pies.

Bake at 425 degrees F for 10 minutes; then reduce heat to 325 degrees F and bake 40 minutes.

PUDDINGS AND CUSTARDS

CRANBERRY CRUNCH PUDDING

Yield: 100 servings (3 pans, 12x22x2 inches each)

Ingredients:

    Topping (below)
  2 No. 10 cans whole cranberry sauce
  1 No. 10 can apples
1 1/4 cups butter

Mix together cranberry sauce and apples. Spread on bottom of 3 prepared pans. Cut butter into chunks and dot on surface throughout. Spread topping over pudding mixture.

Bake at 375 degrees F for 35 minutes. Garnish with cold whipped cream, ice cream, or dollop of creamy sour cream. Serve warm or cold.

TOPPING

3/4 gallon brown sugar
1 gallon less 2 tablespoons flour
1/4 cup baking powder
12 eggs, beaten
1 tablespoon salt
1/4 cup cinnamon
3 cups grated sharp cheddar cheese

Blend topping ingredients together until crumbly.

SURPRISE CHOCOLATE CAKE 'N' PUDDING

Yield: 100 to 120 servings (4 pans, 12x20x2-1/2 inches each)

Ingredients:

Topping (below)
6 pounds flour (or 6 quarts)
7 ounces baking powder (or 1 cup)
2 ounces salt (or 4 tablespoons)
8 pounds sugar (or 4 quarts)
12 ounces cocoa (or 3 1/2 cups)
16 ounces dry milk (or 4 cups)
12 ounces butter, melted (or 3 cups)
8 ounces vanilla (or 1/2 cup)
6 pounds water (or 12 cups)

Mix dry ingredients together. Add melted butter or shortening, vanilla, and water. Mix thoroughly. Put 6 pounds of batter in each pan.

Sprinkle 1 pound, 10 ounces of topping over each pan. Slowly pour 1 quart of water over each of the 4 pans. Bake at 350 degrees F for 25 to 30 minutes.

Top with a dab of whipped cream and chopped nuts.

TOPPING

5 1/3 pounds brown sugar (or 4 quarts)
20 ounces cocoa (or 6 cups)
4 pounds water (or 4 quarts)

Mix brown sugar and cocoa together.

SNOW PUDDING

Yield: 216 servings (4 cobbler pans) or 216 individual molds

Ingredients:

> Whipped Topping (below)
> Raspberry Sauce (below)

- 1 cup plain gelatin
- 2 cups cold water
- 3 1/2 quarts sugar
- 4 1/2 quarts milk
- 2 1/2 cups finely chopped coconut

Soften gelatin in water (about 5 minutes). Heat sugar and half of the milk (2 1/4 quarts) in double boiler until hot; add gelatin. Dissolve gelatin in hot mixture, then add remaining milk. Allow mixture to congeal until it is the consistency of egg whites. When set, whip on machine; add coconut. Combine with 3 1/2 gallons of whipped topping.

WHIPPED TOPPING

- 2 No. 10 cans Rich's whipped topping base plus 1 can cold water (or 9 quarts nondairy whip topping)
- 4 cups powdered sugar
- 1/2 cup vanilla

Whip on medium speed until thick, beat on high speed to get final volume.

RASPBERRY SAUCE

- 6 packages Danish Dessert mix
- 12 cups cold water
- 1 bucket raspberries (or 1 No. 10 can or 3 quarts)

Mix together and heat to boil; continue boiling until mixture thickens. Add pinch of salt and red food coloring. Remove from heat. Add raspberries. Cool.

FRUIT CRISP AND TOPPING

Yield: 54 servings (1 cobbler pan, 12x22x2 inches, cut 6x9)

Ingredients (Apple):

Topping (below)
1 1/4 No. 10 cans apples with juice
3 1/2 cups sugar
1/3 cup cornstarch
1 teaspoon cinnamon
1/8 teaspoon nutmeg
1/4 cup lemon juice
1/4 cup margarine, melted

Ingredients (Apricot):

Topping (below)
1 1/4 No. 10 cans apricots with juice
1 cup crushed pineapple
3 cups sugar
1/3 cup cornstarch
1/2 teaspoon almond extract
1/4 cup lemon juice
1/4 cup margarine, melted

Ingredients (Fruit Cocktail):

Topping (below)
1 1/3 No.10 cans fruit cocktail with juice
2 cups sugar
1/2 cup cornstarch
1 teaspoon cinnamon
1/4 cup lemon juice
1/4 cup margarine, melted

Grease large cobbler pan. Portion fruit into pan, cutting apples into pieces if necessary.

Combine remaining ingredients in order given. Mix well. Sprinkle dry ingredients over fruit and gently blend together.

Sprinkle topping (about 1/2-inch thick layer) over fruit mixture. Serve with whipped cream, ice cream, or another favorite topping.

Bake at 350 degrees F for 1 hour. Sprinkle with topping.

TOPPING

> 2/3 cup margarine, melted
> 1 quart flour
> 1 quart brown sugar
> 1 teaspoon cinnamon
> 1 1/2 tablespoons baking powder
> 1/3 quart bread crumbs or quick oats or combination
> coconut (optional)

Mix dry ingredients together in large bowl; combine with half of the melted margarine. When well mixed, add remaining margarine. There should be no large lumps in mixture.

STRAWBERRY SHORTCAKE PUDDING

Yield: 108 servings (2 pans, 13x9 inches each, cut 6x9)

Ingredients:

> 2 cups miniature marshmallows
> 4 cups frozen sliced berries in syrup, thawed (or 4 packages, 10 ounces each)
> 2 packages (3 ounces each) strawberry Jello
> 4 1/2 cups flour
> 3 cups sugar
> 6 tablespoons baking powder
> 2 cups milk
> 2 cups shortening
> 1 teaspoon salt
> 6 eggs
> 2 teaspoons vanilla

Grease bottom of baking pans. Sprinkle marshmallows evenly over bottoms. Combine thawed strawberries and syrup with dry gelatin and set aside.

In large mixing bowl, combine remaining ingredients. Blend at low speed until moistened. Continue beating at medium speed until well blended. Pour batter over marshmallows.

Bake at 350 degrees F for 45 to 50 minutes. Serve warm or cold with ice cream or whipped cream.

BLACKBERRY SHORTCAKE PUDDING: Substitute blackberries for strawberries. Excellent!

LEMON COCONUT PUDDING

Yield: 108 servings (2 cobbler pans, 12x22x2 inches each, cut 6x9)

Ingredients:

              5 cups margarine
             10 cups brown sugar
             10 cups flour
              5 teaspoons soda
              5 teaspoons salt
             10 cups wheat flakes (Wheaties)
              5 cups coconut
              2 No. 10 cans lemon pie filling
            1/2 cup lemon juice
              2 cups water
            1/2 teaspoon salt
              9 eggs

Combine first 7 ingredients in order given to make crumbs for crust and top. Reserve small amount of crumbs for topping; divide remaining crumbs between cobbler pans. Pat into bottoms of pans.

In separate bowl combine remaining ingredients for lemon filling. Spread over top of crumb crust. Sprinkle reserved crumbs over top of filling.

Bake at 350 degrees F for 40 minutes.

FANTASTIC APPLE MACAROON TORTE (PUDDING)

Yield: 64 servings (1 pan, 16x16 inches, cut 8x8)

Ingredients:

             12 eggs (or 2 cups)
              9 cups sugar
          3 3/4 cups flour
              5 tablespoons baking powder
              3 teaspoons salt
              4 tablespoons vanilla
              3 quarts chopped apples
          1 1/2 quarts chopped nuts

Beat eggs until fluffy. Add sugar and continue beating until fluffy. Sift together dry ingredients and add to eggs and sugar. Fold in vanilla, apples, and nuts.

Pour into prepared pan and bake at 375 degrees F for 50 to 60 minutes. Cut into squares. Serve with vanilla sauce, apple cider sauce, or whipped cream.

NOTE: Recipe can be doubled or tripled easily.

ALMOND DREAM

Yield: 90 servings

Ingredients:

- 5 pounds sugar
- 5 cups water
- 5 cups egg yolks
- 1 tablespoon plain gelatin
- 2/3 cup cold water
- 5 quarts cream, whipped
- 2 quarts almonds, sliced and toasted
- 2 quarts macaroon (coconut) crumbs
- 4 tablespoons plus 1 teaspoon vanilla

Boil water with sugar to soft ball stage. Pour slowly over beaten egg yolks while stirring vigorously. Return to heat and bring to boil, stirring constantly.

Soak gelatin in cold water for 5 minutes. Add to egg yolk mixture, stirring until well mixed. Cool.

When above mixture has thickened, gently fold in remaining ingredients. Freeze.

Serve in pretty dishes or glass stemware. Garnish with toasted chopped almonds or macaroon crumbs and cherry.

BAKED CUSTARD

Yield: 100 servings

Ingredients:

      5 1/2 cups sugar
          1 teaspoon salt
         40 eggs, beaten
          1 quart cold milk
          8 quarts half-and-half, scalded
        1/4 cup vanilla
          1 tablespoon nutmeg

Combine sugar and salt with beaten eggs; slowly add cold milk. While stirring constantly, beat in scalded half-and-half. Pour into custard cups or into shallow baking pans. Place in hot water baths. Sprinkle nutmeg over top. Bake at 325 degrees F for 45 minutes or until knife blade, inserted in custard 2 inches from side of pan, comes out clean.

BAKED FRENCH CUSTARD: Increase sugar by 1/2 cup. Omit nutmeg, sprinkle top with brown sugar, drizzle with maple syrup, and place under broiler until bubbly.

BAKED CARAMEL CUSTARD: Pour 6 ounces caramelized sugar on bottom of each baking pan before adding custard mixture. To serve, invert individual custards to let caramel run down sides.

SPANISH ORANGE DREAM

Yield: 100 servings

Ingredients:

          2 cups plain gelatin
          2 gallons milk
          4 pounds sugar
         32 eggs, separated
          5 quarts orange juice
        1/2 cup orange rind
          1 cup lemon juice
          2 teaspoons salt
        1/4 cup rum

Soften gelatin in 4 cups milk for 5 minutes. Heat remaining milk. Dissolve gelatin in hot milk. Add sugar and mix well.

Beat egg yolks until light; pour hot milk into yolks, beating vigorously. Cook over double boiler until mixture thickens and coats spoon. Remove from heat; add juices and orange rind. Cool.

Beat egg whites with salt and rum until stiff. Fold into custard mixture. Pour into glass stemware, allowing 4 ounces per glass. Garnish with orange twist. Chill.

SWEDISH RICE PUDDING

Yield: 1 pan, 13x22x2 inches

Ingredients:

- 1 pound rice
- 1/2 ounce salt
- 2 1/4 quarts milk
- 1 1/2 quarts water
- 2 1/2 ounces butter
- 1 1/2 pounds sugar
- 1/2 ounce vanilla
- 1 pound eggs
- cinnamon
- nutmeg

Cook first 4 ingredients over low heat until rice is soft. Add butter and set aside to cool.

Mix sugar with vanilla and eggs. Fold into cooled rice mixture. Pour into cobbler pan; place pan in a shallow hot water bath. Sprinkle top of rice with nutmeg or cinnamon or both.

Bake at 375 degrees F for 45 minutes. Stir gently, then bake for remaining 15 minutes or until set.

ROCKY ROAD PUDDING

Yield: 108 servings (2 pans, 12x22x2 inches each, cut 6x9)

Ingredients:

    2 No. 10 cans prepared chocolate pudding
    1 gallon whipped topping
    1 gallon miniature marshmallows
  3 1/2 cups chopped nuts
  5 1/2 cups chocolate chips
    1 cup plain gelatin
  1 1/3 cups cold water

Soak gelatin in cold water for 5 minutes, then dissolve in double boiler over hot water. Cool but do not allow gelatin to set.

Add whipped topping to chocolate pudding; whip. Add gelatin and mix thoroughly. Fold in marshmallows, nuts, and chips.

Spread in pans. Garnish with more chopped nuts. Do not smooth. Refrigerate overnight to set.

BLACK RASPBERRY FLUFF

Yield: 128 servings (1/2 cup each)

Ingredients:

  2 1/2 gallons black raspberry Jello*
  1 1/2 gallons whipped cream
       sugar
       vanilla
       chopped nuts
       Maraschino cherries

Prepare raspberry Jello according to package directions. Allow Jello to set, then whip well. Whip cream; add sugar and vanilla to sweeten and flavor it. Combine Jello with whipped cream. Pour into parfait glasses, molds, or pans. (Before serving, portion fruit Jello in molds or pans into single servings.) Top with whipped cream or whipped cream cheese. Garnish with chopped nuts and a cherry.

Any flavor of fruit Jello can be successfully substituted.

INDEXES

INDEX OF RECIPES

INDEX OF MEDITATIONS AND PRAYERS